The COMPANIONS in Christ™ Network

www.companionsinchrist.org

So much more!

Companions in Christ offers leaders *so much more* than just printed resources. It offers an ongoing LEADERSHIP NETWORK that provides:

- Opportunities to connect with other churches who are also journeying through *Companions in Christ*
- Helpful leadership tips and articles as well as updated lists of supplemental resources
- Training opportunities that develop and deepen the leadership skills used in formational groups
- A staff available to consult with you to meet the needs of your small group
- An online discussion room where you can share or gather information
- Insights and testimonies from other *Companions in Christ* leaders
- A FREE 48-page *Getting Started Guide* filled with practical tools to help you start a group in your church
- FREE *Companions in Christ* posters to use as you promote the group in your congregation

Just complete this card and drop it in the mail, and you can enjoy the many benefits available to leaders through the *Companions in Christ* NETWORK!

- ❏ Add my name to the *Companions in Christ* NETWORK <u>mailing list</u> so that I can receive ongoing information about small-group resources and leadership trainings.
- ❏ Add my name to the *Companions in Christ* NETWORK <u>email list</u> so that I can receive ongoing information about small-group resources and leadership trainings.
- ❏ Please send me a FREE 48-page *Getting Started Guide.*
- ❏ Please send me FREE *Companions in Christ* posters. Indicate quantity needed: _____

Name: _____

Address: _____

City/State/Zip: _____

Church: _____

Email:_____ Phone: _____

D1597142

WOGLG

Fold here and tape.

For information about *Companions in Christ* visit

www.companionsinchrist.org

BUSINESS REPLY MAIL
FIRST-CLASS MAIL PERMIT NO. 1540 NASHVILLE TN

POSTAGE WILL BE PAID BY ADDRESSEE

COMPANIONS in Christ.

UPPER ROOM MINISTRIES
PO BOX 340012
NASHVILLE TN 37203-9540

COMPANIONS
in Christ

The Way of Grace

LEADER'S GUIDE

Marjorie J. Thompson and Melissa Tidwell

UPPER
ROOM BOOKS®
NASHVILLE

COMPANIONS IN CHRIST: THE WAY OF GRACE
Leader's Guide
Copyright © 2004 by Upper Room Books®
All rights reserved.

The Upper Room® Web site http://www.upperroom.org

UPPER ROOM®, UPPER ROOM BOOKS® and design logos are trademarks owned by the Upper Room®, Nashville, Tennessee. All rights reserved.

Unless otherwise stated, scripture quotations are from the New Revised Standard Version Bible, copyright © 1989 by the Division of Christian Education of the National Council of the Churches of Christ in the U.S.A. Used by permission. All rights reserved.

Scripture quotations designated KJV are taken from the King James Version of the Bible.

Scripture quotations marked (NIV) are taken from the HOLY BIBLE, NEW INTERNATIONAL VERSION. NIV. Copyright 1973, 1978, 1984 by International Bible Society. Used by permission of Zondervan Publishing House. All rights reserved.

Scripture quotations designated THE MESSAGE are taken from *The Message* by Eugene H. Peterson, Copyright © 1993, 1994, 1995, 1996, 2000. Used by permission of NavPress Publishing Group. All rights reserved.

"Greenless Child" from *Reaching for Rainbows* by Ann Weems. © 1980 Ann Barr Weems, used by permission of Westminster John Knox Press. Not to be duplicated without written permission from Westminster John Knox Press, 100 Witherspoon Street, Louisville, KY 40202.

Selections from "The Mother of Learning" from *Orphaned Wisdom: Meditations for Lent* by Michael E. Moynahan. Copyright © 1990 by Michael E. Moynahan. Used with permission of Paulist Press. www.paulistpress.com

Prayer based on the *Didache*. Used by permission of Melissa Tidwell.

Cover design: Bruce Gore
Design and implementation: Lori Putnam
Cover art: Carter Bock
Cover art rendering: Marjorie J. Thompson
First printing: 2004

Library of Congress Cataloging-in-Publication

Thompson, Marjorie J., 1953–
Companions in Christ: the way of grace: leader's guide / Marjorie J. Thompson and Melissa Tidwell.
     p. cm.
    Includes bibliographical references.
    ISBN 0-8358-9879-2
    1. Grace (Theology)—Study and teaching. 2. Spiritual formation. 3. Church group work. I. Tidwell, Melissa. II. Title.
BT761.3.T48 2004
253' .7—dc22   2003025104

Printed in the United States of America

For more information on *Companions in Christ*
call 1-800-972-0433 or visit www.companionsinchrist.org

Contents

Weekly Needs at a Glance

Review this Weekly Needs at a Glance list to familiarize yourself with items needed at the *Way of Grace* Preparatory Meeting and the other weekly meetings. Knowing well in advance the items required for each meeting will help you avoid last-minute crises.

Weekly Materials

ALL MEETINGS

- Christ candle (large white pillar candle) or other central candle (such as the Companions Circle of Friends Candleholder) and cloth for worship table
- Hymnals, songbooks, or other arrangements for music (tapes/CDs and player)
- Extra Bibles
- Group ground rules developed during your Preparatory Meeting, printed on newsprint and posted in your meeting room
- "Candle Prayer," printed on newsprint and posted in your meeting room (if you choose to use this prayer as a group):

Light of Christ
Shine on our path
Chase away all darkness
and lead us to the heart of God.
Amen.

- Newsprint and markers or chalkboard/whiteboard
- Optional: Symbol on worship table for link with a partner group (consider a smaller candle or perhaps a postcard or gift from the partner group)

PREPARATORY MEETING

- Participant's Book for each person
- Several copies of the Companions *Journal* for those who may wish to purchase one
- Group ground rules written in advance on newsprint or chalkboard (pages 17–18)
- A copy of the "Holy Listening Exercise" and "Review Questions" (pages 31–32) for each participant
- Printout from the Web site www.companionsinchrist.org (*The Way of Grace* groups area)
- Card titled "Prayers for Our *Companions in Christ* Group" from the back of this Leader's Guide

WEEK 1   COMPANIONSHIP FOR THE JOURNEY

- Blank sheets of newsprint or paper for each participant
- Markers of various colors
- "Exodus Life Map" (page 38) sketched out in advance on newsprint or individual copies for each member
- Closing benediction (page 37) printed on newsprint or a copy for each participant

WEEK 2   COME AND SEE

- A copy of the worksheet "Where Do I 'Live'?" (page 44) for each participant
- Two reflection questions (page 42) on newsprint for use in "Deeper Explorations"
- Closing litany (page 43) printed on newsprint or a copy for each participant

WEEK 3   THE GIFT OF RENEWAL

- A copy of the worksheet "Nicodemus's Journal" (page 49) for each participant

WEEK 4   BEING FULLY KNOWN

- Art supplies (paper and crayons, pastels, or colored pencils)
- Tape/CD of gentle rainfall or waterfall (not ocean waves or thunderstorm) or a tabletop fountain

- Pitcher of water
- A paper cup for each group member
- Closing prayer (page 55) printed on newsprint or copied for each participant

WEEK 5   THE WILL TO BE WHOLE
- Oil for anointing

Option 1
  - Large, round shallow container for water to place on table
  - Small waterproof stand for Christ candle (optional)
  - Small floating candles (two per person)
  - Matches
  - A few small hand towels

Option 2
  - Large, blue bedsheet (flat) or blue plastic tablecloth
  - Several candles
  - Matches
  - Cushions

WEEK 6   THE NEED FOR INTERCESSION
- A copy for each participant of the "Four Scenarios" handout (page 70)
- A copy for each participant of "*Lectio* on Life" worksheet (page 71)
- Instructions and questions (page 67) printed on newsprint
- One cushion comfortable to kneel on

WEEK 7   SEEING AND SAYING THE TRUTH
- A copy for each participant of the handout titled "The Man Born Blind: A Dramatic Reading" (pages 78–80)
- A copy for each participant of the worksheet titled "Blindness, Healing, and Speaking the Truth" (page 81)

Week 8   From Death to Life

- A cross for the worship table (optional)
- Extra facial tissues
- Closing affirmation (pages 86–87) printed on newsprint or copied for each participant

Week 9   The Gift of Restoration

- Group refrain to the "Opening" prayer (Psalm 80:3; pages 90–91) printed on newsprint
- Closing benediction (page 94) printed on newsprint
- A large table with chairs for the Love Feast
- Tablecloth, fresh or dried flowers
- Several baskets or plates for loaves of bread
- A large basket or tote bag for donated food items
- Easily served form of fish (dried/smoked fish, canned sardines, tray of cooked shrimp)
- Dates, grapes, figs, or honey
- Water or juice
- Breadboard and knife
- Paper plates, cups
- Toothpicks or utensils (depending on foods you select)

Acknowledgments

The original twenty-eight week *Companions in Christ* resource grew from the seeds of a vision long held by Stephen D. Bryant, editor and publisher of Upper Room Ministries. It was given shape by Marjorie J. Thompson, then director of the Pathways Center of Upper Room Ministries and currently spiritual director to the *Companions in Christ Network*. The vision, which has now expanded into the Companions in Christ series, was realized through the efforts of many people over many years. The original advisors, consultants, authors, editors, and test churches are acknowledged in the foundational twenty-eight week resource, as well as in the second title of the series, *Companions in Christ: The Way of Forgiveness*. We continue to owe an immense debt of gratitude to each person and congregation there named.

Companions in Christ: The Way of Grace is the fourth title in the series that began with the foundation of *Companions in Christ*. Like its predecessors, *The Way of Forgiveness* and *The Way of Blessedness*, it represents a shorter small-group resource intended to expand on the experience of participation in the twenty-eight week Companions resource; but it may be used prior to experiencing the *Companions in Christ* resource. The progression for the nine-week journey through *The Way of Grace* and the writing of the weekly articles in the Participant's Book are the primary work of John Indermark. The daily exercises in the Participant's Book are the primary work of John Indermark and Stephen Bryant. The material in the Leader's Guide represents the work of a staff advisory team comprised of Stephen Bryant, Lynne Deming, Cindy Helms, Tony Peterson, Robin Pippin, Marjorie Thompson, and Melissa Tidwell. The "Deeper Explorations" were developed by Melissa Tidwell and Marjorie Thompson. In addition, several *Companions* trainers led test groups in their congregations or ministry settings that have offered valuable insight and guidance for developing *The Way of Grace*. The trainers and congregations represented by their groups included Carol Brown, Belmont United Methodist Church, Nashville, Tennessee; Wendy Bryant, St. Johns United Methodist Church, Kingman, Arizona; Marilyn Dickson, First Christian Church, Grand Prairie, Texas; Frank Granger, First Baptist Church, Athens, Georgia; WG Henry, First United Methodist Church, Hartselle, Alabama; Ron Lagerstrom, The Bread of Life Spiritual Formation Center, Davis, California; Deb Suess, Spokane Friends Church, Spokane, Washington; Vicki Walker, Hyde Park United Methodist Church, Tampa, Florida; Jim Hamblen, Pilot Mountain Baptist Association, Winston-Salem, North Carolina; and Larry Peacock, Malibu United Methodist Church, Malibu, California.

Introduction

Welcome to *Companions in Christ: The Way of Grace*, a small-group resource designed to help your small group explore and experience more deeply the grace of God at work within common patterns of growth and change in the Christian journey. *The Way of Grace* follows a series of encounters with Jesus by various characters in the Gospel of John. Together these encounters explore key movements in spiritual formation. Grace predominates in each encounter, even as it does in our personal journey of faith in company with Christ. The stories from John's Gospel thus provide a way for group members to connect the biblical witness with their own experience of God's grace.

In response to small groups who want to continue their exploration of spiritual practices that began with the original twenty-eight-week *Companions in Christ* resource, the Companions in Christ series is being developed. *The Way of Grace* is the fourth title in the series. Earlier titles in the series are *The Way of Forgiveness* and *The Way of Blessedness*. Although it is the fourth title in the series, we commend starting with *The Way of Grace* just after completing the original *Companions in Christ* resource.

Each resource in the Companions series expands on the foundational content of the twenty-eight-week resource and uses the same basic format. The foundational resource, *Companions in Christ*, explored the Christian spiritual life under five headings: Journey, Scripture, Prayer, Call, and Spiritual Guidance. Each supplementary volume of the Companions in Christ series explores in greater depth some aspect of one of these primary categories of spiritual practice.

The Way of Grace falls under the general heading of Journey. The stories in each week's reading follow the chronological journey of Jesus' ministry as presented in John's Gospel.

More importantly, the encounters explored in each story invite group members to reflect on significant turning points, crises, and openings in their own spiritual journeys. As in previous *Companions* resources, the approach to scripture is more formational than informational. While scripture provides the context for each chapter's theme, this is not a Bible study in any traditional sense. We will focus on how these stories touch our hearts, move our wills, and shape our spirits to conform more fully to the life of Christ.

About the Resource and Process

Like all resources in the Companions in Christ series, *The Way of Grace* has two primary components: (1) individual reading and daily exercises throughout the week with the Participant's Book and (2) a weekly two-hour meeting based on directions in the Leader's Guide. The Participant's Book has a weekly article that introduces new material and five daily exercises to help participants reflect on their lives in light of the article's content. These exercises help participants move from information (knowledge about) to experience (knowledge of). An important part of this process involves keeping a personal notebook or journal in which participants record reflections, prayers, and questions for later review and for reference at the weekly group meeting. The daily exercise commitment is about thirty minutes. The weekly meeting includes time for reflecting on the past week's exercises, for moving into deeper experiences of spiritual growth, and for engaging in group experiences of worship.

The material in *Companions in Christ: The Way of Grace* covers a period of ten weeks, a preparatory meeting followed by nine weeks of content with the following themes:

1. *Companionship for the Journey*: The journey of faith takes place in community with one another and with God, who seeks us with grace in Jesus Christ.

2. *Come and See*: God calls us by name to come and see where a more intimate relationship with Christ will lead us.

3. *The Gift of Renewal*: God breaks open to us the possibilities of new birth through free-moving Spirit and grace-filled love.

4. *Being Fully Known*: God knows us wholly and helps us to know ourselves in the light of Christ's love, enabling us to know more of God's reality and truth.

5. *The Will to Be Whole*: The healing God would offer us waits graciously upon our willingness to be made whole.

6. *The Need for Intercession*: The gracious intercession of Jesus Christ on our behalf beckons us to intercede for the sake of others.

7. *Seeing and Saying the Truth*: God calls us to witness to what our faith sees and experiences of Jesus Christ, even in difficult circumstances.

8. *From Death to Life*: The journey of faith does not deny or avoid death but moves through lament into authentic hope and trust in God's grace.

9. *The Gift of Restoration*: Even when we fall or fail, Jesus Christ graciously takes the initiative to restore us to intimacy with God and service in Christ's name.

The Companions in Christ Network

An added dimension of *Companions in Christ: The Way of Grace* is the Network. While you and your group are experiencing *The Way of Grace*, groups in other congregations will also be meeting. The Network provides opportunities for you to share your experiences with one another and to link in a variety of meaningful ways. In the Preparatory Meeting you will be asked to pray for another group, send greetings or encouragement, or receive support for your group. Connecting in these ways will enrich your group's experience and the experience of those to whom you reach out.

The Network also provides a place for sharing conversation and information. The *Companions* Web site, www.companionsinchrist.org, includes a discussion room where you can offer insights, voice questions, and respond to others in an ongoing process of shared learning. The site lists other *Way of Grace* groups and their geographical locations so you can make contact as you feel led. Locations and dates for Leader Orientation training events (basic one-day trainings) and the Leader Training events (advanced three-day trainings) are posted here.

The Role of the Small-Group Leader

Leading a group for spiritual formation differs in many ways from teaching a class. The most obvious difference is in your basic goal as group leader. In a class, you have particular information (facts, theories, ways of doing things) that you want to convey. You can gauge your success at the end of the class if participants demonstrate some grasp of the information. In a group for spiritual formation, your goal is to enable spiritual growth in each group member. You work in partnership with the Holy Spirit, who alone can bring about transformation of the human heart. Here gaining wisdom is more important than gaining knowledge, and growing in holiness is more important than gaining either knowledge or wisdom. Success, if it has any meaning in this context, will be evident over months and even years in the changed lives of group members.

Classes tend to be task-oriented. Groups for spiritual formation tend to be more process-oriented. Even though group members will have done common preparation in reading and daily exercises, group discussions may move in directions you do not expect. You will need to be open to the movement of the Holy Spirit and vigilant in discerning the difference between following the Spirit's lead and going off on a tangent. Such discernment requires careful, prayerful listening—a far more important skill in your role as group leader than talking.

Finally, classes have as their primary focus some set of objective data: a Bible passage, information from a book, or analyses of current events. A group for spiritual formation, however, focuses on the personal faith experience of each group member. Each person seeks to understand and be open to the grace and revelation of God. When group members have read and reflected on a scripture passage, the basis for group discussion is not "What did the author intend to say to readers of that time?" but "How does this passage connect to my life or illuminate my experience?" Discussion centers around a sharing of experience, not a debate over ideas. You will model this type of personal sharing with your group because of your involvement in all parts of the group meeting. The type of leadership needed differs from that of a traditional church school teacher or small-group facilitator. As leader, you will read the material and complete the daily exercises along with other members and bring your responses to share with the group. You will lead by offering your honest reflections and by enabling the group members to listen carefully to one another and to the Spirit in your midst.

Leading a group for spiritual formation requires particular qualities. Foremost among these are patience and trust. You will need patience to allow the sessions to unfold as they will. Spiritual formation is a lifelong process. Identifying visible personal growth in group members over the course of *The Way of Grace* may be difficult. It may take a while for group members to adjust to the purpose and style of a formational group process. As a group leader, resolve to ask questions with no "right" answers in mind and to encourage participants to talk about their own experience. Setting an example of sharing your experience rather than proclaiming abstract truths or talking about the experiences of other well-known Christians will accelerate this shift from an informational approach to a formational process. Trust that the Holy Spirit will indeed help group members to see or hear what they really need. You may offer what you consider a great insight to which no one responds. If it is what the group needs, the Spirit will bring it around again at a more opportune time. Susan Muto, a modern writer on spiritual formation, often says that we need to "make space for the pace of grace." There are no shortcuts to spiritual growth. Be patient and trust the Spirit.

Listening is another critical quality for a leader of a spiritual formation group. This does not mean simply listening for people to say what you hope they will say so you can reinforce them. Listen for what is actually going on in participants' minds and hearts, which may differ from what you expect after reading the material and doing the weekly exercises yourself. While you listen, jot down brief notes about themes that surface. Does sharing center around a particular type of experience? Is a certain direction or common understanding emerging—a hint of God's will or a shared sense of what group members found helpful? What do you hear again and again? What action might group members take together or individually to respond to an emerging sense of call?

A group leader also needs to be accepting. Accept that group members may have had spiritual experiences quite unlike yours and that people often see common experiences in different ways. Some may be struck by an aspect that did not impress you at all, while others may be left cold by dimensions that really move you. As you model acceptance, you help foster acceptance of differences within the group. Beyond accepting differences, you will need to accept lack of closure. Group meetings rarely tie up all the loose ends in a neat package. Burning questions will be left hanging. You can trust the Spirit to bring resolution in time, if resolution is needed. Also be prepared to accept people's emotions along with their thoughts and experiences. Tears, fears, joy, and anger are legitimate responses along this journey. One important expression of acceptance is permission-giving. Permit group members to grow and share at their own pace. Let them know in your first meeting that while you want to encourage full participation in every part of the process, they are free to "opt out" of anything that makes them feel truly uncomfortable. No one will be forced to share or pray without consent. "Where the Spirit of the Lord is, there is freedom" (2 Cor. 3:17).

It is particularly important to avoid three common tendencies:

1. *Fixing.* When someone presents a specific problem, you may be tempted to find a solution and "fix" the problem. Problem-solving generally makes us feel better. Perhaps it makes us feel wise or helps to break the tension, but it will not help the other to grow.

Moreover, we might prescribe the wrong fix. If you or another group member has faced a similar problem, speak only from your own experience.

2. *Proselytizing.* You know what has brought you closer to God. Naturally you would like everyone to try it. You can offer your own experience to the group, but trying to convince others to follow your path is spiritually dangerous. Here is where your knowledge and wisdom come into play. Teresa of Ávila wrote that if she had to choose between a director who was spiritual and one who was learned, she would pick the learned one. The saint might be able to talk only about his or her own spiritual path. The learned one might at least recognize another person's experience from having read about it. Clarifying and celebrating someone else's experience is far more useful than urging others to try to follow your way.

3. *Controlling.* Many of us are accustomed to filling in silence with comment. We may be tempted to think we should have an appropriate response to whatever anyone says; that is, we tend to dominate and control the conversation. Here again, patience and listening are essential. Do not be afraid of silence. Your capacity to be comfortable with silence allows you to be a relaxed presence in the group. If you really cannot bear a long silence, break it with an invitation for someone (maybe one who has been quiet so far) to share a thought, feeling, or question rather than with a comment of your own.

If this style of leadership seems challenging or unfamiliar to you, please seriously consider attending a leader training event for *Companions in Christ.* While leadership training is not required to use this resource, it is highly recommended and strongly encouraged.

Expectations for the "Opening" and "Sharing Insights" Sections of Each Meeting

This section offers a basic process for the first hour of your group session. The first step in the group session is prayer and a time of quiet centering. Invoking the Holy Spirit's guiding presence is especially important in the "Opening" portion of the weekly group meeting (see "A General Outline of Each Group Meeting," pages 18–21).

Most of the "Sharing Insights" part of the group session will focus on individual members discussing their experiences with the daily exercises. Members should bring their journals to refresh their memories of the week's exercises. As the leader, you will generally want to model by beginning with your own reflections, which sets the tone for the rest of the group. Speak briefly (two to three minutes) in order to allow ample time for others to share. Above all, specifically relate one of your responses to a daily exercise. If your sharing is general or abstract, other participants will be less likely to share personal experiences. Your initial offering in this part of the group meeting is one of your most important roles as a leader. Consider carefully each week what you would like to say, remaining mindful of the role your words can play in establishing group trust and the serious intent of this part of the meeting.

You may also describe and model for the group an approach sometimes called "sharing to the center." The Christ candle is set in the middle of the group as a reminder that Christ is truly the center of all that the group members do and say in this meeting. The living Christ, through the presence of the Holy Spirit, mediates personal sharing. Therefore participants can share with one another in God's presence by keeping a general focus on the candle. This focus lessens the need to keep constant eye contact with other participants, which makes the revealing of deeply personal responses less difficult. The practice also helps the group to sense that God is truly the one with healing answers and guiding solutions, not us.

During the "Sharing Insights" time, your main job is to listen. Listen primarily for themes—similar experiences that suggest a general truth about the spiritual life, common responses to the readings that might indicate a word God wants the group to hear, or experiences that might offer practical help to other group members as they try to hear and respond to God's call. Take simple notes so you can lift up these themes as the "Sharing Insights" time comes to an end. You will also ask other group members to share any themes or patterns they may have identified from the discussion. Listen too for key differences in participants' experiences and affirm the variety of ways God speaks to and guides each one of us. Be alert to participants' temptation to "fix" problems, control conversation, or proselytize. Gently remind them to share only their own experiences or responses. The same guidance applies if a participant mentions someone else, whether in the group or outside it, as an example. Nothing can destroy group trust more quickly than exposing confidences.

By establishing up front some ground rules for group sharing, you may avoid problems. In the Preparatory Meeting, you will explain the various components of each week's meeting. Discuss the nature of this sharing time and establish some basic ground rules for the group. Here are some suggestions:

• Speak only for yourself about beliefs, feelings, and responses.

• Respect and receive what others offer, even if you disagree.

• Listen more than talk. Avoid cross talk, interrupting, speaking for others, or trying to "fix" another person's problems.

- Honor the different ways God works in individuals.

- Do not be afraid of silence. Use it to listen to the Spirit in your midst.

- Maintain confidentiality. What is shared in the group stays in the group. If spouses or close friends are in the same group, they will want to establish outside of meeting time mutually agreeable boundaries to their personal sharing in the group.

- Recognize that all group members have permission to share only what and when they are ready to share.

You may want to add to this list before you discuss it with the group.

A few minutes before the scheduled end of the "Sharing Insights" time, state aloud any themes you have noted during the session: a summary report on what you have heard, not a chance to "get in the last word." Make it fairly brief: "I noticed that several of us were drawn to a particular passage. I wonder if God is trying to call our attention to something here." This is a time for summarizing and tying together some themes that have already surfaced.

Finally, you may want to close this part of the session with prayer for the deepening of particular insights, for the ability to follow through on the themes or guidance you have heard, for God's leading on questions that have been left open, or for particular situations that have been mentioned. And you may want to invite all group members who are willing to offer simple sentence prayers of their own.

A General Outline of Each Group Meeting

The weekly group meetings will typically follow the outline explained below. Within the outline are two overall movements: one emphasizes sharing insights and learnings from the week's reading and daily exercises; the other develops a deeper understanding of spiritual disciplines or practices. The first movement, "Sharing Insights," is described in the preceding section. The second part of the meeting, called "Deeper Explorations," may expand on ideas contained in the week's reading, offer practice in spiritual exercises related to the week's theme, or give participants time to reflect on the implications of what they have learned for their own journeys and for the church. It may include a brief look forward if special preparation is needed for the coming week.

Both movements are intended as times for formation. The first focuses on the group members' responses to the weekly reading and exercises. The second focuses on expanding and deepening the week's theme experientially. Some participants may respond more readily to one part of the weekly meeting than the other. For example, one person may write pages of journal responses to the daily exercises and be eager for the "Sharing Insights" time but express reticence in joining a group process for the "Deeper Explorations." Another person who has had difficulty reflecting on daily exercises may have little to say during the "Sharing Insights" time but receive great energy and joy from participating in an experiential learning process later in the meeting. Such variations of response may reflect personality types, while other differences may reflect circumstances or life stages in a person's journey. Be patient, accepting, and encouraging of the fullest level of participation each group member can offer.

Consider carefully the setting for your group meetings. An adaptable space is important for group process. One helpful arrangement is a circle of comfortable chairs or sofas. Or participants might want a surface for writing or drawing. Since the group will sometimes break into pairs or triads, plenty of room to separate is also important. The space for meeting will need to be relatively quiet and peaceful.

A visual focus for the group is important, especially for opening and closing worship times. Some weeks you are free to create this focus in whatever way you choose, perhaps simply with a candle on a small table in the center of the circle.

OPENING (10 MINUTES)

This brief time of worship will give group members a chance to quiet down and prepare for the group session to follow. Each group will eventually discover what works best for its members. The Leader's Guide offers specific suggestions; but if you desire, you can develop your own pattern of prayer and centering. Possibilities for this opening worship include (1) singing a hymn together, or listening to a selected song on tape or CD; (2) silence; (3) lighting a candle; (4) scripture or other reading; (5) individual prayer, planned or extemporaneous; or (6) group prayer using a written or memorized prayer.

SHARING INSIGHTS (45 MINUTES)

The content for this part of the meeting comes from the weekly reading and from participants' responses to the five daily exercises they have completed since the last meeting. If members fail to read the material or skip the daily exercises, they will be left out. If too many come unprepared, the group process simply will not work. Group discussion generally will follow the model given above under "Expectations for the 'Opening' and 'Sharing Insights' Sections of Each Meeting." Since the "Opening" has provided prayer and centering time, this section begins with sharing from you as the group leader, continues with group interaction, and ends with a summary you feel is helpful, followed by a brief prayer. You will need to keep an eye on the time in order to bring the sharing to a close and have time for the summary and prayer.

BREAK (10 MINUTES)

Group break time serves important physical, mental, and relational purposes. It also gives some time for snacking if you arrange for someone to provide food. Do not neglect adequate break time, and be sure to take a break yourself as leader.

DEEPER EXPLORATIONS (45 MINUTES)

This part of the group meeting builds on material in the weekly reading and daily exercises. The content is designed to help group members explore in greater depth the weekly theme, generally through scriptural meditation, prayer, creative process, personal reflection, and sharing. This segment of the meeting is very important, resembling the experiential part of a spiritual retreat in miniature and requiring your thoughtful preparation if you are to guide the process comfortably. Please review the leader material early in the week prior to the meeting so that you have time to think through the process and complete any preparation. **Note:** You may need to lengthen your meeting time in Week 8 "Deeper Explorations," especially if you lead a large group. You may even need an extra meeting. Take this need into consideration as you plan ahead.

CLOSING (10 MINUTES)

As it began, the group meeting ends with a brief time of worship. First you may need to attend to practical matters of meeting place or provision of refreshments if these vary from week to week. You may also have the group draw names for prayer partners for the coming week and ask for prayer requests.

The Leader's Guide includes specific suggestions for the "Closing." Designed to follow closely from the "Deeper Explorations," they may include symbolic acts or rituals of celebration and commitment.

Concluding Matters

Song or hymn selections for the "Opening" and "Closing" times need careful consideration. Review the hymnals or songbooks available to you, and look for singable tunes with thematically appropriate words. If your group sings reluctantly, locate several audiocassette tapes or CDs to play and invite "sing-alongs" or enjoy simply listening.

The Leader's Guide suggests songs for each meeting. A number of these come from a songbook entitled *The Faith We Sing* (TFWS), published by Abingdon Press. This recommended resource is ecumenical in scope. It contains songs that represent several worship styles; it is small, portable, and easy to obtain; most songs in it are simple and singable. Abingdon Press now offers a CD with musical accompaniment to every song in the book. (See the Annotated Resource List in the Participant's Book.) We encourage your group to consider this music resource, while recognizing that each group will have access to different songbooks and may have its own preference. The Participant's Book (pages 126–27) includes a song written specifically for *Companions in Christ* called "Companion Song." It provides annotations both for piano and guitar accompaniment. The music is easy to learn, and the song could serve as a theme song for your group. Try it in your Preparatory Meeting and use it several times during the early meetings. If the group likes it, participants will ask to sing it regularly through these weeks together.

The purpose of the Companions in Christ series is to equip persons of faith with both personal and corporate spiritual life practices that will continue long beyond the time frame of any particular resource. Participants may continue certain disciplines on their own or carry some practices into congregational life. Others may desire the continuation of a small group. As you guide your group through this journey, you may discover that certain subjects or practices generate interest and energy for further exploration. Some group members may wish that certain readings or weekly meetings could go into more depth. When the group expresses strong desire to continue with a particular topic or practice, take special note of it. A number of possibilities exist for small-group study and practice beyond this resource. Some suggested resources are listed on pages 111–19 of the Participant's Book. The group will need to decide future directions toward the end of this experience.

Our prayer for you as a leader is that the weeks ahead will lead you and your group deeper into the wise and mysterious ways of God's grace at every turn in your journey. May your companionship with Christ and with one another be richly blessed!

Preparatory Meeting

The Leader's Guide to *Companions in Christ: The Way of Grace* directly addresses you, the leader, as it presents the material for each group meeting. In places the Leader's Guide offers suggested words for you to speak to the group as a way of introducing various sections. Where this occurs, the words are printed in a bold typeface (such as the first item under "Set the Context"). These words are only suggestions. Feel free to express the same idea in your own words or to adapt as you deem necessary. Remember to speak at a deliberate pace. Whether giving instructions or offering prayers, not rushing your words communicates a sense of peace and grace.

When instructed to guide a reflection process, you will often see ellipses (…). These marks indicate pauses between your sentences to allow participants to ponder them. You will need to develop your own sense of timing in relation to the overall time frame for the guided meditation. Generally fifteen to thirty seconds are sufficient for each pause. In some cases, the text will recommend specific times for certain pauses.

The Leader's Guide assumes that groups are new to the Companions in Christ resources and provides complete explanation of all aspects of the journey. For example, in the Preparatory Meeting participants carefully review the daily and weekly rhythm and are introduced to the printed resource. If your entire group has experienced *Companions*, feel free to abbreviate familiar material and focus on this resource's distinctive aspects and your group's process. One exception is the "Holy Listening Exercise," which is part of this Preparatory Meeting. A review of deep listening, central to spiritual formation, can benefit even an experienced group. Upper Room Ministries encourages leaders to include this experience.

PREPARATION

Prepare yourself spiritually. Review the Introduction to the Participant's Book for *The Way of Grace*, as well as the Introduction in this Leader's Guide. Look over the Contents page in the Participant's Book so you can answer basic questions about weekly topics. Pray for each group member and for the beginning of this journey together along *The Way of Grace*. Pray also that the Holy Spirit will guide you in your role as leader so that the group might begin this time together with genuine openness to receiving and sharing God's grace.

Prepare materials and meeting space. Set up chairs in a circle with a center table and Christ candle or other candle. Make your meeting space inviting and visually attractive. Have a copy of the Participant's Book for each person and several copies of the Companions *Journal* for those who may wish to purchase one. You will need copies of the handouts titled "Holy Listening Exercise" (page 31) and "Review Questions" (page 32); a marker and flip chart or other large piece of paper with group ground rules written out in advance; a print-out from the "Way of Grace Groups" area of the Web site www.companionsinchrist.org that lists groups with whom you may wish to partner (search for a group by city, state, country, denomination, or other key word; while at the site, add your group to the list as available to others looking for a partner); and the card "Prayers for Our Companions in Christ Group" (in the back of this Leader's Guide). Secure hymnals or songbooks. Select the hymns/songs you want to use for the "Opening" and "Closing."

Review the intent of this meeting: to gain a clear grasp of the purpose and process of *The Way of Grace*, to have the opportunity to express questions and hopes concerning this journey, and to review and adopt group ground rules.

OPENING (10 MINUTES)

Welcome all participants by name as they enter. Be sure that each participant has a copy of the Participant's Book for The Way of Grace *and the* Journal *or a notebook.*

Set the context.

- This meeting will prepare us for a new adventure called *Companions in Christ: The Way of Grace.*

- This small-group experience in spiritual formation takes us on a nine-week journey through portions of John's Gospel. We will be guided by eight biblical characters (or groups of characters) who discover God's grace in their encounters with Jesus.

- As we journey together, we too will have many opportunities to discover deeper dimensions of God's grace. We will share insights and explore new ways of seeing God's active presence in our lives—both personally and in the settings of our common life.

Provide a brief overview of the Preparatory Meeting.

- — A chance for group members to introduce themselves
- — Opening worship similar to what they will experience in the "Opening" of each weekly meeting
- — Discussion of the group process
- — Discussion of group members' responsibilities
- — An experience in "Holy Listening"
- — Closing worship similar to what they will experience in the "Closing" of each weekly meeting

Ask participants to introduce themselves.

- Ask participants to introduce themselves by saying their name and a few words about what drew them to this group.

- As leader, model by introducing yourself first. Keep your comments brief and simple to encourage others to do likewise.

Join together in worship.

- Invite the group into a spirit of worship: **Many traveling companions will accompany our journey over these next few months. In addition to one another, we will share this journey with characters from John's Gospel, with other small groups across the country using** *The Way of Grace,* **and with The Upper Room Living Prayer Center, whose volunteers will be praying for us. Above all, we share this journey with Christ our living Lord. As we begin our time together, let's open our hearts to receive the grace of Christ present with us now:**

- Light a candle as a symbol of Christ's presence in your midst. Say words like these: **O Lord, we light this candle to remind us of your presence with us along** *The Way of Grace.* **Help us to hear your voice and respond to your guidance. Amen.**

- Encourage a posture of receptive listening as you read Psalm 81:13: "**O that my people would listen to me.**"

- Pause, then read this phrase again. Ask participants to recall a time when they listened attentively to or for God. Allow a minute of quiet. Then ask them to identify in a word or phrase what prompted such attentive listening and to note this in their journals.

- After another minute, invite everyone in turn to say his or her word or phrase aloud. As leader, model by sharing first.

- Indicate that attentive listening is a critical element of spiritual formation and there-fore central to *The Way of Grace.* As we learn to listen at ever deeper levels to one another and to God, we discover the depths of divine grace. To help participants develop their listening skills, group members will have an opportunity to experience later in this meeting a practice called "Holy Listening."

- Conclude with a spontaneous prayer or with these words: **Gracious God, as we jour-ney through** *The Way of Grace,* **open our hearts that we might be aware of your presence with us in gratitude and trust. In Jesus' name. Amen.**

PRESENT THE RESOURCES AND GROUP PROCESS (10 MINUTES)

Make sure each participant has a copy of the Participant's Book. Go over the Introduction with group members so that each person understands the process of reading, daily exer-cises, and journaling, as well as the outline for each group meeting. Here are some items you will want to mention:

Basic flow of the week. Each participant reads the article for the week on Day 1 (the day after the group meeting) and works through the five daily exercises over Days 2 through 6. The group meets on Day 7. Encourage participants' faithfulness to the process. In preparation for the group meeting, suggest that after Exercise 5 they read over their notebook or jour-nal entries for that week.

Basic flow of a group meeting. Explain the various components: "Opening," "Sharing Insights," "Deeper Explorations," and "Closing." Summarize for the group the explanatory material found in "A General Outline of Each Group Meeting" on pages 18–21 of the Introduction in this Leader's Guide.

Materials for each meeting. Ask the members to bring their Bible, Participant's Book, and journal to each meeting. Because use of the Bible is part of the daily exercises, encourage them to use a favorite modern translation.

EXPLAIN PARTICIPANT RESPONSIBILITIES (15 MINUTES)

Emphasize the importance of each member's commitment to the daily exercises and practices in making the group process work. If some members have not experienced this type of daily reflection or group interaction, they may need help in feeling comfortable with them. Remind participants: **One of the ways we listen to God is by putting our experiences into words. Throughout the week, we record these experiences in our journal. In the group meeting, we articulate our recorded experiences. Both processes offer clarity and new perspective.**

Present the process of journaling.
Note that some participants may already be experienced in the practice of journaling. Call the group's attention to pertinent points from the material on pages 10–12 of the Participant's Book about the value of recording reflections in a journal or personal notebook. Assure them that the writing can be as informal and unstructured as they want. Because each person keeps notes that are most helpful for him or her, the journal becomes the personal record of the spiritual growth that this resource is designed to encourage.

Consider the commitment of listening.
Another important commitment group members make is to listen to and value the words of others: **As companions together, we give full attention to what God is doing in the life of the one speaking. We learn to listen with our heart as well as our head and to create an accepting space in which all can freely explore their spiritual journeys.** The group becomes a place for deep listening and trusting in God's guiding presence.

DISCUSS COMMON GROUND RULES (15 MINUTES)

Ground rules are explained fully on pages 17–18 in the Introduction to this Leader's Guide. The rules suggested there should prove helpful, but as leader you might be prepared to offer other possible rules appropriate to the group. You will also want to allow members to make suggestions. Write the completed list on newsprint for the group to see. Remember that the goal is not a formal agreement or covenant but recognition of the basic rules that are essential in order for the group to deepen its faith and to mature as a community.

INTRODUCE THE *COMPANIONS IN CHRIST* NETWORK AND PRAYER CONNECTIONS (5 MINUTES)

Although we focus on what is happening in our group, we remember that many other groups across the country are participating in *The Way of Grace* also. We can choose to communicate with one of these groups in a way that strengthens our bond in the body of Christ. We have two opportunities to connect with others:

- *Correspondence with other groups.* Referencing the list you printed from *The Way of Grace* groups on the Companions Web site, encourage your members to select and partner with a group, perhaps communicating through notes of greeting and encouragement, or by sending a small love-gift. Use the preparatory meeting as a time to determine how you will proceed with this partnership. You might ask for a volunteer to guide its development.

- *The Upper Room Living Prayer Center* and its network of prayer volunteers will begin to hold your group in prayer. Simply fill in and mail the card titled "Prayers for Our *Companions in Christ* Group" that is bound into the Leader's Guide. Complete the leader's portion of the card by providing your name and your church's mailing address. Please do not use a post office box number. Ask each member of the group to sign his or her first name as evidence of the group's desire to be connected to the larger network of persons involved in *Companions in Christ*.

BREAK (10 MINUTES)

DEEPER EXPLORATIONS (35 MINUTES)

Introduce the "Holy Listening Exercise." (5 minutes)

- This exercise will give everyone a chance to practice prayerful or holy listening, the heart of spiritual friendship and an important element in formational experiences such as the Companions in Christ series. This listening practice is essential to all formational settings: formal or informal, one-on-one, or in a group.

- Ask the group members to pair up for the exercise.

- Give everyone the "Holy Listening Exercise" and "Review Questions" handouts. Explain the process to the group.

- Assure participants that each person will have the opportunity to be both a listener and a speaker. After the first eight minutes, they will take two minutes to reflect on the review questions. Then they will trade roles. At the end of the second eight-minute session, they again take two minutes to reflect quietly with the review questions. During the last five minutes they will compare their responses to those questions.

Practice holy listening in pairs. (25 minutes)

- Ask pairs to find a space apart quickly in order to make the most of the time.

- Help participants honor the time by ringing a bell or calling out the time after each eight-minute period and by reminding them to take two minutes to reflect on the review questions. Alert the participants at the close of the two minutes of reflection time to change roles.

- After the second listening session and evaluation, encourage each pair to compare notes on the experience for five minutes.

Gather as a group. (5 minutes)

- Call pairs back into the group to share what they have learned about holy listening.

- Close with this affirmation of the exercise: **There is no greater gift one person can give to another than to listen intently.**

CLOSING (10 MINUTES)

Invite the group to a time of quiet reflection. **What are your hopes for the time ahead of us as companions in Christ? . . . What are your anxieties about these next weeks together? . . .Commit both your hopes and fears to God now in silent prayer. . . .**

Offer a brief word of prayer, asking that all might be able to release their hopes and concerns into God's gracious hands. End with thanksgiving for each person and for God's good purposes in bringing this group together.

Close with song. You may wish to introduce the "Companion Song" to your group (printed on pages 126–27 of the Participant's Book) or choose a favorite hymn.

Remind the members of their weekly assignment. On the first day they will read the article for Week 1, "Companionship for the Journey." During each of the next five days they will work through one exercise and record their thoughts in their journal. Be sure all participants know the location and time of the next meeting and any special responsibilities (such as providing snacks or helping to arrange the worship table).

Note: If your group is larger than six persons, let the members know that additional time will be needed for the Week 8 meeting so that they can plan for this in advance. If your group is larger than nine persons, you may need to schedule an additional meeting time (see Preparation for Week 8, page 83). Check calendars now.

Holy Listening Exercise

"Spiritual direction takes place when two people agree to give their full attention to what God is doing in one (or both) of their lives and seek to respond in faith."[1]

The purpose of this exercise is for participants to practice holy listening in pairs.

AS THE SPEAKER

Receive your chance to speak and be heard as an opportunity to explore an aspect of your walk with God during the past week (or day). Remember that you and your friend meet in the company of God, who is the true guiding presence of this time together.

AS THE LISTENER

Practice listening with your heart as well as your head. Create a welcoming, accepting space in which the other person may explore freely his or her journey in your presence and in the presence of God. Be natural, but be alert to any habits or anxious needs in you to analyze, judge, counsel, "fix," teach, or share your own experience. Try to limit your speech to gentle questions and honest words of encouragement.

Be inwardly prayerful as you listen, paying attention to the Spirit even as you listen to the holy mystery of the person before you.

When appropriate and unintrusive, you might ask the other person to explore simple questions such as these:

- Where did you experience God's grace or presence in the midst of this time?
- Do you sense God calling you to take a step forward in faith or love? Is there an invitation here to explore?

HOW TO BEGIN AND END THE CONVERSATION

- Decide who will be the first listener, and begin with a moment of silent prayer.
- Converse for eight minutes; then pause for two minutes so that each person may respond to the "Review Questions" handout in silence.
- Trade roles and converse for eight minutes more; then pause again for personal review.
- Use the last five minutes to compare notes on your experiences and your responses to the review questions.

Review Questions

FOR THE LISTENER

a. When were you most aware of God's presence (in you, in the other person, between you) in the midst of the conversation?

b. What interrupted or diminished the quality of your presence to God or to the other person?

c. What was the greatest challenge of this experience for you?

FOR THE SPEAKER

a. What was the gift of the conversation for you?

b. What in the listener's manner helped or hindered your ability to pay attention to your life experience and God's presence in it?

c. When were you most aware of God's presence (in you, in the other person, or between you) in the midst of the conversation?

Week 1
Companionship for the Journey

PREPARATION

Prepare yourself spiritually. Review the material in the Introduction to this Leader's Guide, especially the sections titled "The Role of the Small-Group Leader" and "Expectations for the 'Opening' and 'Sharing Insights' Sections of Each Meeting." Read the article for Week 1, reflect on each daily exercise, and keep a journal along with the other participants. Pray for the Holy Spirit's guidance as you lead the group through this nine-week journey. Pray for each participant, especially for openness to God's guiding presence as the group prepares to explore together *The Way of Grace.*

Prepare materials and the meeting space. As you prepare for each group meeting, refer to "Weekly Needs at a Glance" which begins on page 5 of this guide. Review the items listed under the heading "All Meetings" as well as the items listed under this week's title, "Companionship for the Journey." You will need a Christ candle or other candle to serve as a focal point for your worship table. If you wish to introduce the "Candle Prayer," preprint it on newsprint and post it in a visible place in the meeting room. Also display the ground rules agreed to during the Preparatory Meeting. If your group elected to have a partner group, arrange to share any communication with that group or ideas for doing so. As you complete your daily reflections, pay special attention to Daily Exercises 1 and 2, which will provide key background material for the "Deeper Explorations." Depending on the room space and arrangement for the "Deeper Explorations," you may choose to post on the walls a blank sheet of newsprint for each participant or to give each person an individual blank sheet for table or lap drawing. Have plenty of markers of various colors on hand. Sketch out in advance the "Exodus Life Map" (page 38) on a piece of newsprint, or make a copy for each participant. You may print the closing benediction in advance on a sheet of newsprint or make a copy for each member. Decide how to divide the time between drawing life maps and sharing them: a smaller group may want more time for individual reflection/drawing since you will have more time per person for sharing. Select songs to sing or recorded music to play for the "Opening" and "Closing."

Review the intent of this meeting: that participants will see afresh their lives as a spiritual journey and will be drawn to a deeper desire and commitment to mature in Christ.

OPENING (10 MINUTES)

Welcome all participants by name as they enter.

Set a context.

Welcome to *The Way of Grace.* **Over the next eight weeks, we will accompany eight biblical characters or groups of characters who discover God's grace through their encounters with Jesus. Before sharing their experiences, we will begin this week by reflecting on our own lives and perhaps discovering afresh God's grace in our encounters with Jesus.**

Join together in worship.

- Light the candle at the center of the group. As you light it, ask participants to join you in reciting the "Candle Prayer"; or welcome Christ's presence with words such as these: **The light of this candle reminds us that Christ is present with us now as we gather to begin this new venture, just as Christ is present throughout our life journey.**

- Read Ephesians 2:8 aloud at an unhurried pace: **"By grace you have been saved through faith, and this is not your own doing; it is the gift of God."**

- Ask participants to ponder these words as you read the passage again. Suggest that as they ponder, they identify a gift of God—a grace they have received during this past week. Tell them they will have an opportunity to name their gift if they so choose.

- Read the passage again, leaving a minute or two for reflection.

- Invite members to share briefly the grace identified.

- Offer a prayer of thanks.

- Sing a song. Suggestions: "Grace Alone" (TFWS) or a song of your choosing

SHARING INSIGHTS (45 MINUTES)

In this part of the meeting, group members will identify and share where they have experienced God's presence in their lives this past week. Begin by reminding group members of the theme for this week—experiencing grace on the journey.

1. Give participants time to review briefly the article for this week and their journal entries for the daily exercises, noting parts of the article or daily exercises that they found especially meaningful. Ask participants to pay particular attention to their journaling in response to the first two daily exercises. (*5 minutes*)

2. Ask group members to share insights from the weekly reading and their journal entries. Focus the sharing as much as possible on faith journeys (the first two daily exercises). This exchange will help prepare group members to draw their spiritual life maps in the "Deeper Explorations" portion of today's meeting. As leader, model the sharing by offering your brief reflections first. Encourage deep and active listening. If the group numbers more than eight, you may want to form two groups to ensure that everyone can participate in the sharing. (*35 minutes*)

3. With the whole group, note the main points or common themes that emerged from the sharing. What refrains or echoes were evident in these reflections? (*5 minutes*)

BREAK (10 MINUTES)

DEEPER EXPLORATIONS (45 MINUTES)

Help group members explore and share parts of their spiritual journey through life maps.

Set a context. (1 minute)

The spiritual journey is about the growing role of faith in the whole of life. We can't really separate the spiritual part of our journey from the rest of our lives—the ordinary ups and downs of daily living.

In our "Deeper Explorations" time now we will look at some events of our lives using what we'll call a life map. This brief sketch of our life can help us learn something of one another's spiritual journeys.

Illustrate a life map. (2 minutes)

Direct everyone's attention to the "Exodus Life Map" on the newsprint or handout. Indicate that this is an example of a life map that depicts key moments and movements in the life of the Israelites at a crucial time in their formation as a people. While not portraying their entire life story, the Exodus represents an intensely challenging faith pilgrimage early in the Israelites' history. Make several points from this illustration:

1. Most important to note in a life map are major events rather than places, although places may signify events.

2. A life map can be as simple as this illustration; it need not be detailed or proportionally accurate.

3. We may choose to illustrate an especially important segment of our life rather than the whole.

Draw life maps. (10–15 minutes)

Provide plenty of colored markers so participants can choose several to depict their journey if they wish. Participants will either stand at newsprint posted on the walls of the meeting room or sit with paper before them on a table or their laps. Instruct the group with words such as these:

Take the next ten (or fifteen) minutes to think about your life as a journey. Sketch a map or diagram that depicts several key moments and turning points in your pilgrimage. You might show movement along your path by drawing U-turns, forks in the road, circles, mountains, deserts, or rivers. Gaps might represent parts of life not remembered. Where the terrain changes, you may want to write a word or draw a symbol to represent its meaning. Remember that you may choose to depict a particular segment of your life rather than all of it.

Share our journeys. (25–30 minutes)

After group members have finished their maps, ask them to explain briefly up to three of the events they have depicted. Depending on the size of the group, each person will have only three to five minutes to share. Remind participants that they will have more time to talk with each other in depth as the weeks progress.

Reflect on the common ground of our journeys. (2 minutes)

Ask the group to spend a few moments reflecting quietly on the similarities and differences represented in these diagrams. Invite continued quiet reflection as you ask, **What do you hope for as this group begins to journey through *The Way of Grace* together?**

CLOSING (10 MINUTES)

Paraphrase Mark 1:38. "Jesus said to the disciples, 'Let us go on.'"

Reflect on the journey.

If six months or a year from now you drew your life map again, one of the events likely to be on it would be this *Way of Grace* experience. What is your prayer for this time? What do we need from one another as we set out on the journey?

Invite participants, as comfortable, to speak their prayers.

Close with a responsive benediction.

> Leader: **Godspeed to you and your companions as you set out on this journey.**
>
> Group: In company with one another, and in company with God revealed to us in Jesus Christ, we do not travel alone.
>
> All: We travel the way of grace. Let us go on!

Sing a song of blessing. Suggestion: "I Was There to Hear Your Borning Cry" (TFWS)

Extinguish the candle. As you do so, remind all present to carry the light of Christ within them through this week's journey.

Remind the group of the time and location of your next meeting.

Exodus Life Map

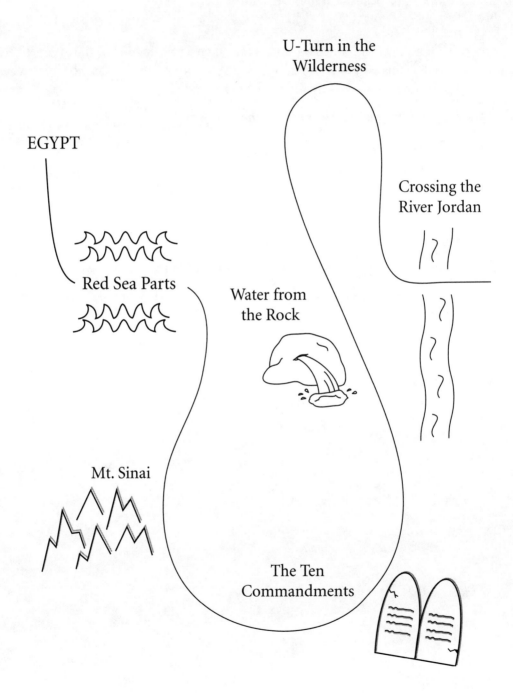

U-Turn in the
Wilderness

EGYPT

Crossing the
River Jordan

Red Sea Parts

Water from
the Rock

Mt. Sinai

The Ten
Commandments

Week 2
Come and See

PREPARATION

Prepare yourself spiritually. If you are new to leading a formational small group, review once more the Introduction to this Leader's Guide, giving special attention to "The Role of the Small-Group Leader" and "Expectations for the 'Opening' and 'Sharing Insights' Sections of Each Meeting." Read the article for Week 2, reflect on all the daily exercises, and keep a journal along with the participants. Pray for your ability as a leader to be open to the guiding presence of God's Spirit through the meeting. Pray also for each participant and for your group as a whole to be open to Christ's invitation to "come and see."

Prepare materials and the meeting space. Refer to "Weekly Needs at a Glance" in the opening pages of this guide. Review the items listed under "All Meetings" as well as under this week's title, "Come and See." Arrange chairs in a circle or around a table. Include a Christ candle or other candle to serve as a focal point for worship. If you use the "Candle Prayer," post it alongside the group ground rules in a visible place. If appropriate, arrange for an update on the most recent communication with your partner group. You will need a copy of the worksheet titled "Where Do I 'Live'?" (page 44) for each participant. Be sure to copy the two reflection questions for pairs or triads (page 42) on newsprint ready to post after the guided meditation. If you lack experience in leading guided meditations, test your pace by reading only the meditation aloud, allowing for the pauses while your own imagination responds, and timing yourself. It should take approximately ten minutes. You may either print out the closing litany on newsprint or make copies for each person. Select songs to sing or recorded music to play for the "Opening" and "Closing."

Review the intent of this meeting: that participants will experience Jesus' invitation to "come and see" where he dwells, discovering their response to that invitation as they explore where they themselves dwell.

OPENING (10 MINUTES)

Welcome all participants as they enter.

Set a context.

This is our second meeting of nine as we journey through *The Way of Grace*. This week we have been reflecting on Jesus' invitation to the disciples to "come and see" who he is and where he dwells. Today we will explore more deeply Jesus' invitation in relation to who we are and where we dwell.

Join together in worship.

- Light the candle in the midst of your worship setting. Bid the group join you in saying the "Candle Prayer," or offer words such as these: **The brightness of this candle reminds us that only the light of Christ can illumine the depths of our hearts.**

- Read this phrase from 2 Corinthians 4:18: **"We look not at what can be seen but at what cannot be seen."**

- Allow a moment for quiet reflection.

- Ask participants to bring to mind situations or relationships where they have needed to look with spiritual eyes to see the goodness of a person or the potential meaning beneath the surface of an event.

- Read 2 Corinthians 4:18 again, allowing another pause for reflection.

- Encourage participants to reflect aloud on the situations or relationships that come to mind. Be prepared to respond first, modeling brevity for the group.

- Close with a song. Suggestions: "Open Our Eyes" or "Cry of My Heart" (both in TFWS)

SHARING INSIGHTS (45 MINUTES)

During the next forty-five minutes, participants will identify and discuss where they have experienced God's presence in their lives during this past week. Begin by reminding group members of this week's theme—exploring the call to discipleship by responding to Jesus' invitation to "come and see."

1. Ask participants to review briefly this week's article and their journal entries in response to the daily exercises. (*5 minutes*)

2. Invite participants to share insights from the article and their journal entries. Offer your own brief reflections first. Encourage the group to practice deep and active listening during this time. (*35 minutes*)

3. Take a few minutes to identify the main points or common themes that have emerged from this time of mutual exchange. What themes occurred more than once, and how did those themes touch the group? (*5 minutes*)

BREAK (10 MINUTES)

DEEPER EXPLORATIONS (45 MINUTES)

Help the group members discover where they "live" in relation to where Christ "lives."

Introduce the theme. (1 minute)

Our "Deeper Explorations" time will help us discover with new clarity the connection between where Jesus lives and where we live. We will start by focusing on our own lives, then move to an imaginative meditation on Jesus' life. Remember that the risen Christ accompanies us in this adventure, so we can go forward with confidence and openness to God's Spirit!

Reflect with worksheet individually. (15 minutes)

Distribute copies of the worksheet titled "Where Do I 'Live'?" Ask participants to find personal space in the room to reflect on the questions and to note responses on the sheet.

Introduce the guided meditation. (4 minutes)

Regather the group with worksheets in hand. Remind the members that Christ remains present with us and that they now have an opportunity to encounter Jesus imaginatively as they explore the relationship between where they live, or dwell, and where he dwells.

Encourage everyone to settle comfortably and to take several slow breaths in preparation for a guided meditation. Center yourself during this time, so you can read the meditation slowly while providing enough "pause time" for personal reflection.

Guide the meditation on encountering Jesus. (10 minutes)

Imagine Jesus entering your current life, appearing a little distance from you in some ordinary place. . . . You begin to move toward him, and your eyes meet his. . . . He asks,

"What do you desire?" Let yourself respond from your depths. What deep desire can you name as you stand in Jesus' presence? ... *(pause for 30 seconds)*

Now Jesus looks at you with great love and asks, "Where do you live?" He wants you to show him where you dwell, in your mind and heart. Are you ready to allow Jesus to "come and see" where you live? ... Think back to your reflection sheet.... Ask Christ to help you look more closely at the words and images connected with your "dwelling place" .... What do you learn as you look with Christ at where you dwell? ...*(pause for 30 seconds)*

Turn to Jesus and ask him, "Where do you dwell?" Hear him respond, "Come and see." Then let Jesus show you something of his true dwelling place—the heart of God.... Ask him to show you how the heart of God sheds light on the unresolved issues of your life.... Note any insights or images that come to you.... *(pause for 60 seconds)*

Now ask Jesus to show you how to move from where you live to where he lives.... Let him show you where you already dwell in him.... Let him show also how he offers you a different place from which to think and feel and act.... Give thanks for what you see.... *(pause for 30 seconds)*

Take a minute now to linger and absorb your experience with this meditation....*(pause for 60 seconds)*

Share in pairs or triads (15 minutes)

- Invite participants to exchange insights with one another, guided by the two questions written on newsprint:
  1. What have you discovered about "where you live" and "where Jesus lives"?
  2. Where is God's invitation to you in this encounter with Christ?

CLOSING (10 MINUTES)

Sing a song or hymn. Suggestions: "The Summons" or "Come and See" (both in TFWS)

Draw attention to the threefold invitation to "see" in John 1:35-51:

- Two of John the Baptist's disciples ask Jesus where he lives. He replies, "Come and see."
- Philip tells Nathanael about Jesus of Nazareth. Nathanael asks if anything good can come from Nazareth. Philip replies, "Come and see."
- Nathanael, discovering that Jesus knows him, proclaims that Jesus is no ordinary man. Jesus tells him he will "'see greater things.'"

Say to the group: **The third invitation is a promise that those who follow Jesus will see amazing things, mysteries of God, the very heavens opened. This promise is also ours as we embark on our journey through** *The Way of Grace.*

Guide a time of prayer. Ask the group to open their hearts and minds to God in prayer, while opening their "inner eye" to what God wants them to "come and see." After a few minutes of silence, bid single-word or short-phrase prayers.

Close with the following litany.

Leader:	"What do you want?" "Actually, lots, but for starters, 'Where do you live?'"
Group:	"Come and see."
Leader:	The perfect bait for catching curiosity and leading salty fisherfolk into the depths of mystery.
Group:	"Come and see."
Leader:	We slowly tiptoed deeper into life and death. His constant response to our timidity that tantalizing challenge:
Group:	"Come and see."
All:	And we went. And we saw more than we could ever have imagined.[1]

Say or sing a benediction.

Where Do I "Live"?

Explore where you tend to "live" on a daily basis. List the feelings, hopes, anxieties, or expectations that have shaped your life recently. (Clues as to where you "dwell" inwardly may be found in what you "dwell on.")

Try sketching an image of this "dwelling place" (face with a smile or frown, overcrowded calendar, a peaceful scene, etc.). Add descriptive words if you wish.

Reflect on unresolved matters in your life, such as deep hopes and concerns or unrealized aspirations. List a few of these and beside each write a word describing what you seek in order to resolve it (clarity, peace, fulfillment, justice, etc.).

Week 3
The Gift of Renewal

PREPARATION

Prepare yourself spiritually. Read the article for Week 3, reflect on each daily exercise, and keep your journal. Pray for the renewing breath of God to fill you so that your guidance of the group meeting will be Spirit-led. Pray for the same Spirit of new life to touch each participant according to his or her need and to prepare all for your group meeting time.

Prepare materials and the meeting space. Refer to "Weekly Needs at a Glance" in the opening pages of this guide, briefly reviewing the list below "All Meetings" and checking items listed under this week's title, "The Gift of Renewal." Arrange chairs in a circle or around a table, with the Christ candle as a worship focal point. You may wish to have the "Candle Prayer" and ground rules posted in a visible place in the room and to arrange for an update on communication with your partner group. Make a copy of the worksheet titled "Nicodemus's Journal" (page 49) for each participant. Select songs and songbooks or recorded music for the "Opening" and "Closing."

Review the intent of this meeting: that participants will discover more fully what they seek from God and what God's gift of spiritual renewal means for them.

OPENING (10 MINUTES)

Welcome all participants as they enter.

Set a context.

Welcome to week three as we journey through *The Way of Grace*. This week, Nicodemus has been our traveling companion. In our meeting we will take a closer look at this religious leader's quest for more in his spiritual life, a journey that led him to seek Christ under cover of night.

Join together in worship.

- Light the candle and ask your group to join you in praying the "Candle Prayer" or offer words such as these: **We light this candle as a reminder of Christ's presence with us and of the renewing action of the Holy Spirit among us. We are on holy ground!**

- Read Psalm 84:1-2:

  "How lovely is your dwelling place,
  O LORD of hosts!
  My soul longs, indeed it faints
  for the courts of the LORD;
  my heart and my flesh sing for joy
  to the living God."

- Ask participants to reflect on these words, recalling a time this past week when they truly longed for God or felt real joy in God's presence. Pause in silence for a minute or so, then invite brief sharing.

- Offer a prayer of thanks.

- Close with a song or hymn. Suggestions: "Holy, Holy, Holy"; "Joy Comes with the Dawn"; "Come Rejoice in God" (all from TFWS)

SHARING INSIGHTS (45 MINUTES)

Encourage participants to identify and speak to where they have experienced God's presence in their lives this past week. Remind everyone of the theme for this week—the need for rebirth and renewal.

1. Instruct participants to review this week's article and their journal entries. (*5 minutes*)

2. Invite them to contribute their insights. As leader, offer your own brief reflections first. Encourage the group to practice deep and active listening to one another. (*35 minutes*)

3. Draw out the main points or common themes that have emerged from these shared reflections. What refrains or echoes were heard? (*5 minutes*)

BREAK (10 MINUTES)

Deeper Explorations (45 minutes)

Guide the group members to reflect on their lives through the story of Nicodemus, to clarify what they seek from Christ and what Christ offers them for the sake of spiritual renewal.

Lay the foundation. (3 minutes)
- Read aloud John 3:1-2. Make a few brief observations about being a seeker: We tend to think of seekers as persons who are inexperienced with faith. But Nicodemus is a leader in his religious tradition. He visits Jesus at night seeking something else, something more than what he already knows. We are all seekers in some way. What else leads us to read and reread the Gospels, to ask faith questions, to pray fervently about our lives? In today's "Deeper Explorations" we will identify with Nicodemus in order to discover more clearly what we ourselves seek from God and what God offers us in response.

Introduce a time of individual reflection with the journal worksheet. (2 minutes)
- Pass out the reflection sheet titled, "Nicodemus's Journal."
- Encourage group members to step into Nicodemus's shoes, imagining from his time and place the nighttime conversation with Jesus and his journal reflections afterward. Ask each participant to find a place apart to complete the worksheet.

Spend individual reflection time with "Nicodemus's Journal." (15 minutes)

Share in triads. (10 minutes)
- Gather the group and form triads (or pairs for smaller groups).
- Encourage triads to talk about their journal reflections with one another by focusing on two questions: As Nicodemus, what were you seeking? What did you find?

Reflect with larger group. (15 minutes)
- Invite each triad or pair to tell the larger group one key insight from their conversation.
- Ask how our way of imagining Nicodemus's life connects with what we ourselves seek from Christ or with what renewal might look like in our own lives.
- Recall that Nicodemus saw in Jesus something beyond what he had received from his faith community. What need for renewal do we see in our faith community, and how might Jesus' response to Nicodemus speak to the larger church?

CLOSING (10 MINUTES)

Sing a song. Suggestions: "Spirit, Spirit of Gentleness" (TFWS) or "Companion Song"

Ask participants to ponder these questions:

- What one question do you most want to ask Jesus—for yourself or your church? *(Allow a minute of silence)*

- What does Jesus reply to you? *(Allow another minute of silence)*

Invite group members to speak what they hear in a word or phrase.

Invite prayers based on these reflections. Be sure to pray for willingness to receive what God is offering through Jesus' challenging wisdom and invitation to renewal.

Remind the group that our expectations of the spiritual life are limited by a human understanding of God and even of ourselves. God wants more for us and for our church than we realize or imagine. The apostle Paul prays that we "may be filled with all the fullness of God" (Eph. 3:19).

Offer a benediction by reading Ephesians 3:20-21.

Nicodemus's Journal

Imagine that you are Nicodemus, coming home after visiting Jesus by night. Your mind and heart are full of thoughts, questions, and anticipation. Write a journal entry to capture the important feelings, insights, or wonderings of this extraordinary night. Use the following questions to guide your imagination:

1. Why did you seek Jesus out; what were you looking for? What did you see in him that you didn't see in your own tradition and training?

2. What do you make of Jesus' response to you? As you ponder and pray to reach the deeper meaning of his mysterious words, what insights emerge?

3. What might you choose to say to your peers in the Jewish council about this man Jesus?

Being Fully Known

PREPARATION

Prepare yourself spiritually. Read the article for Week 4, reflect on each of the daily exercises, and record your responses in your journal. Pray for the grace to be a clear, gentle, and effective leader within the group. Pray also that each participant might be open to the gift of being fully known and loved by God.

Prepare materials and the meeting space. Refer to "Weekly Needs at a Glance," briefly reviewing items listed under "All Meetings" as well as this week's title, "Being Fully Known." Arrange chairs in a circle or around a table with the Christ candle in the center. If appropriate, have the "Candle Prayer" and ground rules visibly posted, and arrange for an update on recent communication with your partner group.

For the second half of the group meeting, you will need art supplies such as paper, crayons, pastels, or colored pencils. To create the sound of running water for the "Closing," secure either a tape/CD of gentle rainfall or a waterfall (not ocean waves or a thunderstorm) or a small tabletop fountain. You will also need a pitcher of water and a cup for each participant, including yourself. Print the closing prayer on newsprint in advance, or type and copy the prayer for each group member. Be sure to select songs and songbooks or recorded music for the worship times. Again, if you lack experience in leading guided meditations, test your pacing by reading the meditation aloud. Although the text suggests pauses, use your judgment about which images or questions need more time for reflection. The meditation should take about ten minutes.

Review the intent of the meeting: that in discovering more deeply the blessing of being fully known and loved, participants may receive the living water offered by Christ.

OPENING (10 MINUTES)

Welcome all participants as they enter.

Set a context.

Welcome to week four in our nine-week journey through *The Way of Grace*. This week we will explore further the grace that is received in being fully known and graciously accepted by God. Our traveling companion is the woman at the well who knows what it means to receive, then offer, the living water of God's love.

Join together in worship.

- Enter a spirit of worship by lighting the candle at the center of your group. Recite together the "Candle Prayer," or offer words such as these: **The light of Christ shines in the darkness, revealing all that we are in the light of God's love. Thanks be to God!**

- In preparing to hear the psalm, encourage those present to set aside all distractions so they can rest in the joy of being fully known, accepted, and loved by God.

- Read at an unhurried pace these verses from Psalm 139:

> O LORD, you have searched me and known me.
> You know when I sit down and when I rise up;
> > you discern my thoughts from far away.
>
> . . . .
>
> Where can I go from your spirit?
> > Or where can I flee from your presence?
>
> . . . .
>
> If I take the wings of the morning
> > and settle at the farthest limits of the sea,
> even there your hand shall lead me,
> > and your right hand shall hold me fast.
> If I say, "Surely the darkness shall cover me,
> > and the light around me become night,"
> even the darkness is not dark to you;
>
> . . . .
>
> I praise you, for I am fearfully and wonderfully made.
> > Wonderful are your works.

- Ask participants to take a few minutes to ponder silently God's intimate knowledge of and deep love for us.
- Sing together. Suggestions: "Loving Spirit" or "Celebrate Love" (both in TFWS)
- Close with a spontaneous prayer of thanksgiving, or offer this prayer: **God of grace, how precious it is to be set free by your knowledge of us! You know every thought and impulse in us, yet always look upon us tenderly, embracing us as cherished children. Surely, your grace knows no bounds. May we allow ourselves to be transformed by your love. We pray in Jesus' name. Amen.**

SHARING INSIGHTS (45 MINUTES)

Encourage group members to name ways in which they have experienced God's presence this past week. Remind them of the theme—receiving the gift of being fully known and deeply loved by God.

1. Let participants review the article and their journal entries for this week. (*5 minutes*)
2. Invite them to contribute their insights. As leader, model the sharing by offering your own brief reflections first. Encourage deep and active listening. (*35 minutes*)
3. Point out any common themes or refrains that you heard during the discussion. Ask, **What might the Spirit be saying to us through these common themes?** (*5 minutes*)

BREAK (10 MINUTES)

DEEPER EXPLORATIONS (45 MINUTES)

Help the group to receive and offer "living water" through a deeper experience of being known and loved by Christ.

Lay the foundation. (2 minutes)

When Jesus met the woman at the well, he seemed to know everything about her. He knew what her life was like and what she really needed—living water. Jesus knows us as deeply as he knew this woman, and he perceives our thirst for fullness of life. In today's "Deeper Explorations" we hope to experience something of the power of living water that Jesus offered the woman at the well. We will reflect on our own spiritual thirst that draws us to the well where we may be fully known by Jesus.

Prepare participants for a guided meditation. (3 minutes)

- Ask the group members to settle comfortably, close their eyes, and take a few slow breaths. After several moments, invite them to open their minds and hearts in a receptive attitude toward God's Spirit.

- Indicate that you will lead them through a meditative reflection to help them connect the Samaritan woman's story with their own lives.

Lead the meditation. (10 minutes)

Jesus said, "Those who drink of the water that I will give them will never be thirsty. The water that I will give will become in them a spring of water gushing up to eternal life" . . . . *(pause for 30 seconds)*

Jesus offers the woman of Samaria "living water," an inward spring that flows through us from God's eternal source. . . . Living water literally meant "moving water," which would be found at the deep well source. Ponder the image of moving water in relation to the dynamic movement of God's Spirit that Jesus promises to us by faith. . . . *(pause for 30 seconds)*

The woman in this story seems unaware of her own thirst. What kind of thirst do you see in her? . . . *(pause for 30 seconds)*

Jesus knows her situation fully yet relates to her with genuine regard, teaching her profound spiritual truths. . . . How do you think this woman felt about being fully known yet treated respectfully and seriously by Jesus? . . . *(pause for 30 seconds)*

What kind of thirst do you perceive in yourself? . . . *(pause for 30 seconds)* When have you felt deeply, perhaps unexpectedly, known by another person? . . . *(pause for 30 seconds)* Ponder something in your life you feel ashamed of, or try to hide. . . . *(pause for 30 seconds)* Consider that Jesus knows you fully—and loves you completely. . . . Does this truth help to meet your thirst? . . . *(pause for 30 seconds)*

As the woman of Samaria receives the "living water" of Christ's love, it starts to flow out of her to others. She calls out to people from her community to "come and see" Jesus. . . . Do you know someone who needs to hear the message: "Come and see the One who knows all of me and still loves me"? . . . *(pause for 30 seconds)* Be aware of thirsty people around you—thirsty physically or emotionally, relationally or spiritually. . . . *(pause for 30 seconds)* How can you offer them the "living water" of God's Spirit, the spirit of love that you have received? . . . *(pause for one minute)*

Reflect on the experience. (15 minutes)

After the minute of silence, ask participants to respond to the guided meditation through journaling or by sketching images that may have come to mind. (Point out art supplies.)

Share responses in the group. (15 minutes)

Gather the group together. Allow a minute or two each for participants to share significant insights from their reflection time, including sketches if they choose.

Closing (10 Minutes)

Create an ambience with the sound of falling water by playing softly a CD of gentle rain or a waterfall or by turning on a small water fountain in the background. (The sound of ocean waves or thunderstorms is not appropriate to the image of the story.)

Read the following words from Mark 9:41: "**Truly I tell you, whoever gives you a cup of water to drink because you bear the name of Christ will by no means lose the reward.**"

Serve a cup of water to each participant.

- Remind the group that the woman of Samaria gradually receives God's living water as she accepts being known and loved by Jesus. With us also, it takes time to accept fully how deeply known and loved by God we are. The truth needs to penetrate many layers inside each of us. Assure everyone that this process is a natural part of the spiritual journey.

- Pour water from a pitcher into a cup for each participant. As you offer it, encourage each one to absorb the truth of God's love, and say a blessing: (**Name**), **you are known and loved by God. Drink of God's living water.** Pause for a moment to allow each person to take in the blessing.

Offer the following prayer together:

> We are born of water and of Spirit.
> We have drunk from the living water.
> We have been baptized into Christ;
> And when we offer even a cup of cold water to those who thirst,
> we offer the living water in his name.
> Thanks be to God!
> Amen.

Sing a song. Suggestions: "Water, River, Spirit, Grace," "Spirit of God," "Where the Spirit of the Lord Is" (all in TFWS), or "Spirit of the Living God"

Offer a brief benediction.

Week 5
The Will to Be Whole

PREPARATION

Prepare yourself spiritually. Read the article for Week 5, reflect on each daily exercise, and record responses in your journal. This week's meeting touches deeply on our desire for healing, so your inner preparation through prayer will be especially important. Pray that the Holy Spirit will guide your leadership and work powerfully in the meeting process toward greater wholeness for all participants.

Prepare materials and the room. Review the "Weekly Needs at a Glance" for items listed under "All Meetings" as well as those listed under this week's title, "The Will to Be Whole." Before arranging the room, read carefully through the two options described under "Deeper Explorations." Prayerfully consider both options and choose one to prepare for, taking into account sufficient space or table size. Place the Christ candle centrally as a focal point for worship and sharing. Post the "Candle Prayer" and ground rules if you need them, and arrange for an update on communication with your partner group. Secure oil for anointing. Select songs and songbooks or taped music to play.

Option 1 in "Deeper Explorations" requires a large, round, shallow container to fill with water and place on a central table. The container should be small enough to fit your table but large enough to accommodate water and twice as many floating candles as you have group participants. You can purchase inexpensive plastic "pottery" at a nursery or the plant section of a discount store. You will also need small floating candles (two per person), matchbooks, and a few small hand towels. If you wish to place the Christ candle in the water, you may need a small waterproof stand. Option 2 requires a large blue bed-sheet (flat) or a blue plastic tablecloth. You will also need several candles, matches, and cushions. Be prepared to lead or teach the refrain to the African American spiritual, "Wade in the Water" (TFWS).

Review the intent of this meeting: that participants explore God's call to become whole and to intercede for one another in willing to be made whole.

OPENING (10 MINUTES)

Welcome all participants as they enter.

Set a context.

This is week five in our nine-week journey through *The Way of Grace*. Our traveling companion this week has been the sick man by the pool at Beth-zatha. In our meeting we will continue to explore our personal desire to be made whole, as well as the call to help others enter the healing waters of God's love through our prayers.

Join together in worship.

- Light the Christ candle and recite the "Candle Prayer," or offer a prayer such as this: **Holy Spirit, living flame of love, may your light guide us to the wholeness of new life in Christ. Amen.**

- Remind the group that the man by the pool knew he needed help from others to get to a place of healing: **One of the chief ways we can help one another toward healing is through intercessory prayer. But sometimes we do not know how to pray for another or for ourselves. The following passage from Romans offers encouragement and the comfort that no matter how stumbling our prayers, the Spirit is already at work interceding on our behalf.**

- Read Romans 8:26-27: **"The Spirit helps us in our weakness; for we do not know how to pray as we ought, but that very Spirit intercedes with sighs too deep for words. And God, who searches the heart, knows what is the mind of the Spirit, because the Spirit intercedes for the saints according to the will of God."**

- Allow a minute for quiet reflection. Encourage the group to ponder the extraordinary compassion of God, who listens to the deepest cry of our hearts even when we cannot put prayer into words.

- Offer a prayer of thanksgiving.

- Close by singing "Spirit of the Living God" or a hymn of your choosing.

SHARING INSIGHTS (45 MINUTES)

Begin by reminding participants of this week's theme—the desire to be made whole.

1. Let participants review the article and their journal entries for this week. *(5 minutes)*

2. Encourage them to share their insights and questions. Offer your own brief reflections first as a model. Remind them to listen attentively. *(35 minutes)*

3. Draw out any common themes from these shared reflections that might be clues to God's word for the group. *(5 minutes)*

BREAK (10 MINUTES)

With help from a few group members, use five minutes of this time to set up the room for "Praying around the Pool" (arrange water container, candles, matches, and towels; or the blue cloth, cushions, candles, etc.).

DEEPER EXPLORATIONS (40 MINUTES)

Help group members support one another's will to be made whole by helping each other into the waters of God's healing love through prayer.

Set a context. (1 minute)

Jesus' question to the man by the pool is one of the great questions of faith: "Do you want to be made well?" The author points out that while the answer to that question seems obvious, we have many subconscious reasons for clinging to illnesses and frailties. Often we need a wider community of faith to assist us; we need caring people who can support our desire to be made well.

Lay the foundation. (1 minute)

The sick man answers Jesus' question by saying, "Sir, I have no one to put me into the pool when the water is stirred up; and while I am making my way, someone else steps down ahead of me." In our "Deeper Explorations" we will become for one another the caring community this man lacked, truly a Christian poolside community. We will symbolically recreate the pool of Beth-zatha and through our prayers, practice helping others into God's healing waters.

Reflect individually. (3 minutes)

Invite participants to think of a person who needs prayers for healing—physical, spiritual, emotional, or relational. Who needs help getting into the pool of God's healing grace? It might be someone who has asked for specific prayers or someone in need who has little support. Since the group will share these prayers aloud, suggest that if confidentiality is a concern they may choose to use only first names or to identify the need generally ("a friend with cancer" or "an aunt with marriage problems.")

Engage together in "Praying Around the Pool." (35 minutes total)

Option 1

Introduce the process and set the stage. (5 minutes)

- Dim the lights in the room if you can, or if your group meets during the day try turning off inside lights and allowing natural daylight to suffuse the room.

- Place a round, shallow container filled with one to two inches of water at the center of the table. Set the Christ candle either at the center (on a small stand) or to one side.

- Distribute two floating candles to each participant, and place several matchbooks around the table, along with a few small hand towels.

- Speak briefly about the symbols: the water symbolizes the pool at Beth-zatha; each candle will represent a person who needs help getting into the healing waters; lighting the candle represents that person's hope or desire to be made whole.

- Explain the process: When a group member lights a candle and puts it in the water, naming aloud the person's name or concern, all the group members will gather around the "pool" and gently stir the water with their fingers as they pray quietly. If someone feels moved to pray aloud for the person named, they may do so. One or two spoken prayers for each person represented by a candle will be enough (you may need to limit this to one if your group is larger than eight). As leader, you will conclude the prayers for each person named by saying, "Lord, in your mercy," to which the group responds, "Hear our prayer." Tell participants to keep their eyes open during these prayers, since lighted candles moving through the water could be hazardous to bare fingers!

- Indicate that the second candle represents their own desire for healing and that they will have an opportunity later to pray for one another's will to be whole.

Pray around the pool. (30 minutes)

- Invite participants to enter into a minute of silence as they reflect on what it means to support one another's will to be whole.

- You might transition to the time of prayer by humming or singing softly together the refrain to the African American spiritual "Wade in the Water" (in TFWS) if participants know it.

- Ask each person to light a candle, place it in the water, and describe briefly the person/situation represented. Offer an example such as: "This candle is for my aunt; the light symbolizes her hope for a whole marriage."

- After the first candle is set afloat, prompt the group members to "stir the waters" by placing their fingers in the "pool" with a gentle stirring motion. Ask everyone to pray quietly that God's Spirit might "stir up" the movement needed to bring wholeness to the person or situation named.

- Allow for silent prayer and for one or two spoken prayers, depending on the size of your group. After the prayer(s), conclude by saying, "Lord, in your mercy. . ." and await the group response, "Hear our prayer."

- After each person has had an opportunity to place a candle in the water, encourage participants to lift their second candle and name a concern for their own healing or wholeness. Ask another group member to take that candle, light it, and place it in the water to symbolize the continued pattern of "helping one another into the pool." Allow time for silent/spoken prayers as before.

Option 2

If you have enough space in your meeting room, give prayerful consideration to this option. It represents a more active and dramatic way to symbolize the healing waters. While it may strike you as a bit awkward at first, the process has proved to be a powerful and effective way of enacting intercessory prayers for healing.

- Turn down lights and set lit candles around the room to create a quiet atmosphere.

- Place a large, blue cloth on the floor to symbolize the pool at Beth-zatha and gather participants around it, seated on chairs or cushions on the floor. Suggest that they take off their shoes as a sign that they are on holy ground.

- If participants are familiar with "Wade in the Water," lead them in singing the refrain several times (you might arrange to teach it before you begin).

- Speak briefly about the gift of being in Christian community and the privilege of praying for one another. Then describe the group process below.

- Invite participants to come one at a time to the center of the "pool," representing the person they have in mind. They may stand, sit, or kneel (provide a chair or cushion, if helpful), then briefly describe the person/situation needing wholeness.

- Ask group members in the surrounding circle to pick up the edges of the cloth and gently ruffle it, "troubling the waters" as they pray silently that God may bring healing to the person in need. Suggest that after a brief silence, one person in the circle pray aloud for the person in need of healing, concluding the prayer by saying, "Lord, in your mercy," to which the group will respond, "Hear our prayer."

- After each person has had the opportunity to stand in the circle representing another, ask if any group members wish to stand in the circle seeking prayers for their own needs. Repeat the process for each participant who comes to the center.

Conclude with prayer.

Whichever option you choose, conclude the time "around the pool" with a prayer that gathers up all concerns voiced, entrusting them to God's gracious care and healing power. Use the following prayer if you wish: **God of all goodness and grace, thank you for this opportunity to intercede for the gift of healing on one another's behalf. Receive all our desires to be made whole, and bless our intentions to help others find their way into your healing presence. We pray in Jesus' name. Amen.**

CLOSING (15 MINUTES)

Gather in a circle without a table.

Reflect briefly on the experience of praying in community. Ask:

- **What was it like to pray this way?**

- **What have we received that we might carry into our personal or communal patterns of prayer?**

Read Romans 8:26-27 again, inviting a few moments for silent gratitude that the Spirit prays in us even when we do not know how to pray.

Introduce the anointing with healing oil.
We have prayed for the healing of others and of ourselves. The Holy Spirit continually prays in us according to God's will for our deepest wholeness. Now if you desire, you may receive a sign of God's grace—an anointing with oil for healing.

Anoint each person around the circle with oil. Speak the following simple prayer as you anoint the forehead and lay a hand on the head of each person:

> **God to enfold you.**
> **Christ to touch you.**
> **The Spirit to surround you.**[1]
> **Amen.**

Sing the refrain to "Wade in the Water" again or the "Companion Song."

Close with a benediction.

Week 6
The Need for Intercession

PREPARATION

Prepare yourself spiritually. Read the article for Week 6, reflect on the daily exercises, and keep your journal. Pray for your deepening compassion as a leader and for each participant's acceptance of Christ's grace and discovery of the freedom to extend it to others.

Prepare materials and the room. Refer to "Weekly Needs at a Glance" to review items listed under this week's title, "The Need for Intercession." Arrange chairs in a circle or around a table, placing the Christ candle as a central focal point. If the group uses the "Candle Prayer," post it alongside the ground rules in a visible place. If appropriate, arrange for an update on recent communication with your partner group. Make copies for each participant of the handout titled "Four Scenarios" and the worksheet "*Lectio* on Life." Print on newsprint the instructions and two questions (page 67)—the second part of the journaling exercise. Secure a comfortable cushion to kneel on. Select songs or recorded music for worship times.

Review the intent of this meeting: that participants practice living in the awareness of Christ's interceding presence and become more alert to daily opportunities for interceding as advocates in our communities.

OPENING (10 MINUTES)

Welcome all participants as they enter.

Set a context.

In week six of our journey through *The Way of Grace*, the woman caught in adultery and her accusers have been our traveling companions. As we explore further Jesus' response of noncondemning grace, we hope to see daily occasions to practice interceding for others with Christlike advocacy.

Join together in worship.

- Light the candle and say together the "Candle Prayer," or offer words such as these: **In lighting this candle, let us remember the light of Christ's presence that illumines our hearts and helps us to view others with noncondemning grace.**

- Read Matthew 11:28-30: **"Come to me, all you that are weary and are carrying heavy burdens, and I will give you rest. Take my yoke upon you, and learn from me; for I am gentle and humble in heart, and you will find rest for your souls. For my yoke is easy, and my burden is light."**

- After a few moments, read the following "saying" from the desert wisdom tradition: **"Abba John the Little said: We have abandoned a light burden, namely self-examination, and taken up a heavy burden, namely self-justification."**[1]

- Invite silent reflection on the following questions, leaving at least thirty seconds of silence after each:

    What burden am I carrying?

    Am I ready to take on the light yoke of Christ?

    Can I receive Jesus' words, "Neither do I condemn you," both for myself and for others?

- After a few minutes of reflection, encourage silent or spoken prayers and conclude with the Lord's Prayer.

- Sing "Freely, Freely"; "Ubi Caritas" (TFWS); or a song of your choosing.

SHARING INSIGHTS (45 MINUTES)

Remind the group of this week's theme—our own need for intercession and how Jesus' noncondemning grace leads us to intercede and intervene on behalf of others.

1. Let participants review the article and their journal entries for this week. *(5 minutes)*

2. Invite them to share their thoughts and insights. Set the tone by offering your own brief reflections first. Encourage deep listening without interruptions. *(35 minutes)*

3. Draw out the common themes from these shared reflections, and ask how the Spirit is speaking to the group through them. *(5 minutes)*

Break (10 Minutes)

Deeper Explorations (45 Minutes)

Guide the group members to expand their understanding and practice of intercession to the communal dimension of intervention and advocacy.

Set a context. (1 minute)
Last week, in relation to the sick man at the pool, we offered prayers of intercession for people in need of healing and wholeness at a personal level. This week, in relation to the woman caught in adultery, we expand on the theme of interceding in the more public sense of intervention or advocacy. As we absorb and believe for ourselves the grace of Jesus' words, "Neither do I condemn you," we can offer the grace of advocating and interceding for others.

Introduce the theme. (1 minute)
Jesus interceded on behalf of a woman caught in the act of sin, putting himself between the woman and her accusers. His intervention clearly signals God's grace for sinners. We want our responses in daily life to resemble more closely Jesus' response. In our "Deeper Explorations" we will consider persons for whom we may be called to intercede in the sense of intervention or advocacy. How, as individuals and as community, might we be called to actively extend God's grace to others?

Introduce reflection time with handouts. (3 minutes)

- Give each participant a copy of the "Four Scenarios" handout and the worksheet titled "*Lectio* on Life."

- Ask group members to read the four scenarios that depict persons in need of compassion and intercession, situations that we might encounter in our everyday life.

- Tell them to journal with the "*Lectio* on Life" worksheet. Post these instructions and questions on newsprint to be done after completing the "*Lectio* on Life" worksheet:

  Reflect on these questions based on the personal situation you identified in Question 2:

  1. Imagine that Jesus appears in the midst of this situation. How does he respond to the person(s) involved?

  2. What difference could it make in your own response if you were truly aware that Christ is present with you and with the other person(s) involved in this situation?

Read and reflect individually with the handout and worksheet. (20 minutes)

Share in the larger group. (20 minutes)

- Gather the group together.

- Invite sharing around the "*Lectio* on Life" worksheet.

  What real-life situations came to mind?

  How do we tend to respond in such situations?

- If such points are not made, you might add a few words such as these: **The situations we've discussed here represent real dilemmas for most of us. Voices and concerns from different angles of each situation offer no easy answers. Sometimes we know what we should do but feel that real obstacles stand in our way or that we don't have the resources and community support we need to respond as well as we might like to.**

- Now ask the group members to reflect on the two questions posted on newsprint: How did they imagine Christ's presence and response in these same situations? What difference did it make to "see" Jesus fully present and active?

- Finally, ask participants to consider how they might live each day more aware of Christ's presence and the summons to actively intercede on behalf of others. What practices have they found valuable, or what could they try?

CLOSING (10 MINUTES)

Assemble the group in a circle with no chairs.

Introduce the prayer process.

- **As Jesus placed himself between the accusing crowd and the woman, we too are called to be the body of Christ interceding for others, including those of us in this group. As we close our meeting, we will gather around each participant and pray for one another—to be fully aware of Christ's presence in the situations we've just shared and to be empowered to intercede in future situations as they arise.**

- Indicate that each participant may come, one at a time, to kneel or stand in the center of the circle (provide a cushion to kneel on). Instruct group members to gather around this person, laying their hands on his or her shoulders.

Call for prayers.

- Christ calls us to intercede and intervene on behalf of others. The Holy Spirit stands ready to empower us for this service. Let us call on the Spirit for such empowerment through prayer, which we will first offer silently for each person. Then, when I speak each person's name, we will say together the following personal benediction: "May you be filled with Christ's presence and power!"

- Allow the group to practice the benediction once as you name a participant. Ask someone to speak your name after the silent prayers when you are in the center of the group.

Invite silent prayers for each person as he or she comes to the center of the group. As a group, offer the benediction to conclude each person's prayer time.

Pray the Lord's Prayer together after all have received personal prayers.

Sing a song. Suggestions: "More Like You" (TFWS) or "Breathe on Me, Breath of God"

FOUR SCENARIOS
Invitation to Intercession

1. **Greenless Child** by Ann Weems

   I watched her go uncelebrated into the second grade,
   A greenless child,
   Gray among the orange and yellow,
   Attached too much to corners and to other people's sunshine.
   She colors the rainbow brown
   And leaves balloons unopened in their packages.
   Oh, who will touch this greenless child?
   Who will plant alleluias in her heart
   And send her dancing into all the colors of God?
   Or will she be left like an unwrapped package on the kitchen table—
   Too dull for anyone to take the trouble?
   Does God think we're her keeper?[2]

2. You are on the church property and grounds committee, which receives a report that a homeless man is sleeping in the recycling container in the church parking lot. Some kids at a recent youth event noticed him crawling into the container and went out to offer him their leftover pizza. One committee member says that he is trespassing and advocates calling the police to move him along. Another member thinks the coming cold weather will drive him away and that we should do nothing. Another wants to take up a collection to rent an apartment for the man. They ask what you think.

3. In the grocery checkout line, you see a Middle Eastern family. The woman wears a robe and head covering, and her husband has a beard. Two young children are with them. They ask to write a check, and the clerk curtly asks for two pieces of identification. After they leave, the clerk asks why we let those people stay in our country after 9/11.

4. You see a casual friend at the gym and begin to chat. Later you notice bruises on her upper arm and neck that she tries to conceal. You have met her husband, who seems to be an angry, controlling person, and wonder if she has been physically abused. A few weeks later, you see this woman and her husband arguing in the parking lot.

Lectio on Life

We have here an opportunity to practice what is sometimes called *lectio* on life. In practicing *lectio divina* with a scripture text, we listen intently for a "nugget" that seems to call out specifically to us. We ask, "What is God trying to say to me just now through this word or phrase?" We reflect deeply, pondering God's personal message. To reflect on our lives with the same prayerful attention is to practice *lectio* on life.

1. Choose one scenario for further reflection that you feel particularly drawn to (refer to the "Four Scenarios" handout). How would you respond in this situation?

2. Ponder how this vignette reminds you of some actual situation you know about or are facing personally. What circumstance in your life is similar to this one? What is your current response to this situation?

Week 7
Seeing and Saying the Truth

PREPARATION

Prepare yourself spiritually. Read the article for Week 7, reflect on each daily exercise, and keep your journal. Pray for wise discernment in your leadership role, as well as for the whole group, that together you might perceive more clearly Christ's healing presence and truth, finding courage to live and speak it.

Prepare materials and the room. Refer to "Weekly Needs at a Glance" to review items listed under this week's title, "Seeing and Saying the Truth." Arrange the room with your worship focus area and Christ candle. Post the "Candle Prayer" and ground rules if you are using them. Arrange to share any recent communication with your partner group. For "Deeper Explorations" you will need copies of two handouts: the handout titled "The Man Born Blind: A Dramatic Reading" (pages 78–80) and the worksheet titled "Blindness, Healing, and Speaking the Truth" (page 81). Be sure to select songs to sing or taped music to play for the "Opening" and "Closing."

Review the intent of this meeting: that participants, like the blind man, will gain new spiritual sight and practice speaking the truth they have come to see.

OPENING (10 MINUTES)

Welcome all participants as they enter.

Set a context.

This is our seventh week of nine as we continue to journey through *The Way of Grace*. This week we have traveled with the man born blind, who received physical and spiritual sight through his encounter with Jesus. We hope to recognize our own blinders and come to see deeper spiritual truths through this meeting time together.

Join together in worship.

- Light the candle in the midst of the group and join in praying the "Candle Prayer" or offer words such as these: **May the light of Christ enlighten our hearts with spiritual sight and shine on our minds with the knowledge of truth.**

- Read Psalm 36:7-9 slowly:

  How precious is your steadfast love, O God!
  All people may take refuge in the shadow of your wings.
  They feast on the abundance of your house,
  and you give them drink from the river of your delights.
  For with you is the fountain of life;
  in your light we see light.

- After a pause, encourage participants to ponder especially the last phrase, "in your light we see light." Ask how they have experienced this truth in their own lives.

- Invite brief spoken prayers.

- Sing a hymn or song of your choice or "O Lord, You're Beautiful" (TFWS).

SHARING INSIGHTS (45 MINUTES)

As group members prepare to share where they have experienced God's presence this past week, remind them of this week's theme—learning to see the truth and to speak it.

1. Let participants review their notes on the article and daily exercises. *(5 minutes)*

2. Invite them to share their insights and questions. You may want to offer your own brief reflections first. Encourage deep and active listening during this time. *(35 minutes)*

3. With the group, gather up any common themes you have noticed, and ponder briefly how the Spirit may be leading you through these refrains. *(5 minutes)*

BREAK (10 MINUTES)

DEEPER EXPLORATIONS (45 MINUTES)

Encourage participants to see themselves more clearly through the story of the man born blind and to discover the workings of God in daily life that reveal truths they can affirm together.

Introduce the theme. (1 minute)

In this meeting we will look more closely at how the story of the man born blind connects with our stories. Then we will consider how this narrative's key questions might help us glimpse the truth-revealing works of God.

Lay the foundation. (1 minute)

We will be reading and role playing the story of the man born blind through a dramatic group reading of the text. As we do so, let's listen carefully for the questions asked by different groups in the story and ponder how their questions are like our questions. How are issues of seeing and saying the truth raised by various characters? Where do we fit into this drama?

Do a dramatic group reading of John 9:1-41. (13 minutes)

- Distribute the handout titled "The Man Born Blind: A Dramatic Reading." Assign a part to everyone in the group (key roles are listed at the top of the handout). As group leader, you might serve as narrator. If your group is small, combine a few roles. If it is larger, have at least two disciples/neighbors and two Pharisees to voice the differing opinions in the text. Give group members a chance to mark their role(s) on the handout. *(3 minutes)*

- Engage in a dramatic group reading of the text. If meeting space allows, encourage participants to act out some of the physical movements of the story. Action will make it a lively and enjoyable experience. *(10 minutes)*

Reflect with worksheet individually. (10 minutes)

Invite participants to reflect on their experience with the dramatic reading, using the questions on the worksheet titled "Blindness, Healing, and Speaking the Truth." This reflection process is designed primarily for individual use. If your group seems energized by the dramatic reading and you think they would benefit from remaining together, let the questions on the worksheet guide a group discussion.

Reflect as a group. (10 minutes)

- Open a group discussion with words like these: **This story revolves around a set of questions asked by various people in the narrative. Three of these are core questions we ask ourselves over and over about suffering, healing, and truth.**

  1. **Who sinned?** (question of suffering and its causes)

2. **Do you believe?** (question of faith in relation to healing)
3. **Are we blind?** (or, **Surely we aren't blind, are we?**) (question of truth)

- Write the three questions above on newsprint or chalkboard. Encourage participants to consider times when they ask these same questions. For example:

  1. "Was your uncle with emphysema a smoker?" (Who sinned?)

  2. "Do you really believe that a prayer vigil for a person with terminal cancer could make a difference?" (Do you believe?)

  3. "Can God welcome a non-Christian believer into the kingdom?" (Are we blind?)

Create an affirmation of faith. (10 minutes)

- Jesus tells the disciples that this man was born blind so that God's works of power might be revealed in him. Ask the group members where they see God's power or truth at work in some of the questions they have asked. For example:

  1. My uncle with emphysema was an amazing witness to patience and faith.

  2. I have seen the healing of a broken relationship in a person we prayed for, even though she was not healed physically of her cancer.

  3. We have begun to see that God works through people we would least expect.

- On newsprint, list some basic faith truths the group can affirm together from their reflections on sin/suffering, faith/healing, and blindness/seeing truth. Write "We believe…" before each statement. These statements need not be polished, only honest.

- Point out that this set of statements represents the group's affirmation of faith, truths the members have discovered that they can speak together in closing worship.

CLOSING (10 MINUTES)

Sing a song. Suggestions: "Be Thou My Vision"; "O Christ, the Healer" (sung to the tune of the "Tallis' Canon"); or a song of your choosing

Read John 9:3-4 or this paraphrase by Eugene Peterson:

> Jesus said, "You're asking the wrong question. You're looking for someone to blame. There is no such cause-effect here. Look instead for what God can do. We need to be energetically at work for the One who sent me here, working while the sun shines." (THE MESSAGE)

Read together the affirmation of faith created by the group.

Close with the Lord's Prayer.

Announce to the group: **Our "Deeper Explorations" next week will rely on the daily exercises done during the week. You will choose how to do the exercises; make every effort to complete the option of your choice.**

Remind the group that next week's meeting may need to be extended, and be sure all are in agreement concerning the time commitment. If you agreed to an extra meeting at the Preparatory Meeting (see page 30), remind the group of that decision.

Say or sing a benediction.

The Man Born Blind: A Dramatic Reading

Based on John 9:1-41

N – Narrator   DN – Disciples/Neighbors   J – Jesus

M – Man born blind   F – Pharisees/the Jews   P – Parents

N: As he went along, Jesus saw a man blind from birth. His disciples asked him,

DN: "Rabbi, who sinned, this man or his parents, that he was born blind?"

J: "Neither this man nor his parents sinned; he was born blind so that the works of God might be revealed in his life. While it is day, we must do the work of him who sent me. Night is coming, when no one can work. As long as I am in the world, I am the light of the world."

N: Having said this, he spit on the ground, made mud with the saliva, and spread it on the man's eyes.

J: "Go, wash in the pool of Siloam."

N: Siloam means "sent." So the man went and washed, and came back able to see! His neighbors and those who had formerly seen him begging asked,

DN: "Isn't this the man who used to sit and beg?"/ "Yes, it is!"/ "No, it only looks like him."

M: "Yes, I am the man! I am the man."

DN: "Then how were your eyes opened?"

M: "The man called Jesus made some mud and put it on my eyes. He told me to go to Siloam and wash. So I went and washed, and then I could see!"

DN: "Where is this man?"

M: "I don't know."

N: They brought the man who had been blind to the Pharisees. Now it was a sabbath day when Jesus made the mud and opened his eyes. So the Pharisees also asked the man how he had received his sight.

M: "He put mud on my eyes. Then I washed, and now I see."

F: "This man is not from God. He does not keep the sabbath."/ "But, how can a sinner do such miraculous signs?"

N: And they were divided. So they turned again to the blind man.

F: "What do you say about him? It was your eyes he opened."

M: "He is a prophet."

N: The Jews did not believe that he had been blind and had received his sight until they sent for the man's parents.

F: "Is this your son, who you say was born blind? How is it that now he can see?"

P: "We know this is our son, and that he was born blind. How it is that he now sees we do not know, nor do we know who opened his eyes. Ask him, he is of age; he can speak for himself."

N: His parents said this because they were afraid of the Jews, for the Jews had already agreed that anyone who confessed Jesus to be the Messiah would be put out of the synagogue. So for the second time, they called the man who had been blind and said to him,

F: "Give glory to God! We know that this man is a sinner."

M: "I don't know whether he is a sinner. I know only one thing: that though I was blind, now I see."

F: "What did he do to you?"

M: "I've already told you, and you wouldn't listen. Why do you want to hear it again? Do you want to become his disciples too?"

F: "You are his disciple, but we are disciples of Moses! We know God has spoken to Moses, but as for this man—we don't know where he comes from."

M: "What an astonishing thing! You don't know where he comes from, and yet he opened my eyes. We know God does not listen to sinners, but only to one who worships him and obeys his will. Never since the world began has it been heard of that anyone opened the eyes of someone born blind! If this man were not from God, he could do nothing."

F: "You were born entirely in sin, and are you trying to teach us?"

N: And they drove him out. . . . Jesus heard they had driven him out, and when he found him, asked,

J: "Do you believe in the Son of Man?"

M: "And who is he, sir? Tell me, so I may believe in him."

J: "You have seen him; the one speaking with you is he."

N: And the man worshiped him.

J: "I came into this world for judgment so that those who do not see may see, and those who do see may become blind."

N: Some of the Pharisees near him heard this and said to him,

F: "Surely we are not blind, are we?"

J: "If you were blind, you would not have sin. But since you say, 'We see,' your sin remains."

Blindness, Healing, and Speaking the Truth
Worksheet for Reflection

What new perspective on the story did you gain by hearing it through the voice of the character(s) you portrayed in the dramatic reading?

According to the person you portrayed, what is the truth about the blind man's healing? What do you imagine this person thinks is true of Jesus?

What barriers exist to this character's seeing or saying the truth?

Step back from identifying with the role you read, and reflect on whom you most naturally identify with in this story, and why.

Week 8

From Death to Life

PREPARATION

Prepare yourself spiritually. Read the article for Week 8, and choose the option you prefer for writing your lament. As you continue to pray for group members, ask God to prepare each and all for the closure of this small group experience over these next two weeks. Pray also that the dynamic promise of our faith may become vividly real for each participant this week as the group shares experiences and feelings regarding death and life.

Prepare materials and the room. Refer to "Weekly Needs at a Glance" to review items listed under this week's title, "From Death to Life." Arrange the room as usual. In addition to the Christ candle in the worship focus area, you may wish to place a cross as a fitting symbol of death and resurrection. Be sure to have extra tissues available. You will also need to write the closing affirmation on newsprint or to type and copy it as a handout. If appropriate, arrange for an update on the most recent communication with your partner group. Select songs to sing or recorded music to play for the "Opening" and "Closing."

Issues of timing are critical in this meeting. The first half of the meeting has been shortened and the second half lengthened. Because of the tender nature of grief, it may take longer for group members to share their laments than one meeting allows for. If you have a small group (four to six), each person may be able to share and receive prayer within the hour allotted in the "Deeper Explorations." If the group is larger than six, you will likely need extended time or even another meeting to complete the process. Even with a small group, ask the members if they are willing to take extra time so as not to rush the process. If they cannot go over the time limit, you will need to determine approximately how long each person may have to share a lament, allowing time after the sharing for the group to pray with each one. Please read the Leader's Note for this week (page 88).

Review the intent of this meeting: that participants will have an opportunity to express a direct, honest lament to God; that participants consider their mortality and come to rest in the gift of knowing by faith that their union with God in Christ is eternal.

OPENING (10 MINUTES)

Welcome all participants as they enter.

Set a context.

Welcome to the eighth meeting in our journey through *The Way of Grace.* **This week, Mary, Martha, and Lazarus have been our traveling companions. As we experience Jesus' presence and response to the death of his friend Lazarus, we come to a fuller knowledge of God's gift of life through Christ.**

Join together in worship.

- Light the candle and join with your group in the "Candle Prayer" or offer words such as these: **The light of this candle reminds us that Christ, our life, is eternally present with us. Thanks be to God!**

- Read Psalm 16:8-11:

    I keep the LORD always before me;
      because he is at my right hand, I shall not be moved.

    Therefore my heart is glad, and my soul rejoices;
      my body also rests secure.
    For you do not give me up to Sheol,
      or let your faithful one see the Pit.

    You show me the path of life.
      In your presence there is fullness of joy;
    in your right hand are pleasures forevermore.

- Invite reflection on this passage, especially the psalmist's sense of gladness, security, and joy in God. Ask, **When have you felt a similar sense of joy or confidence in your faith?**

- Ask willing members to state aloud a word or phrase that conveys their sense of security or gladness in God.

- Close with song. Suggestions: "The Lord's My Shepherd, I'll Not Want"; "Where the Spirit of the Lord Is" (TFWS); or another favorite hymn

- Alert the group to the changes in time frame for the "Sharing Insights" and "Deeper Explorations" portions this week. (Please note instructions below.)

SHARING INSIGHTS (30 MINUTES)

Since you have a shorter time for shared insights, encourage participants during this time simply to reflect on the process of writing their lament. Ask a few questions such as: Did your psalm just pour out of you, or did you struggle to express it? Which psalms were most helpful to you in finding your own voice?

1. Give participants a few minutes to review their journal entries. *(3 minutes)*
2. As leader, model the sharing by offering your own brief reflections on the process of writing a lament. As always, encourage active listening to one another. *(25 minutes)*
3. After all members have shared, identify any common themes that have emerged. *(2 minutes)*

BREAK (10 MINUTES)

DEEPER EXPLORATIONS (60 MINUTES)

Help participants understand loss, grief, and faith through the story of Lazarus and through expressing personal psalms of lament.

Set a context. (2 minutes)

Grief can turn our world upside down. Jesus' willingness to share in our suffering and his power to turn our pain into joy can right our world. In the remainder of our meeting time we will share something of our grief through laments. Perhaps, as Jesus did with us, we will also share in the supportive power of weeping with one another as we move from life to death and from death back to life.

Share psalms of lament. (58 minutes)

- Explain the process of sharing our laments and praying for one another, and indicate a basic time frame for each person's process (see Leader's Note).

- Give participants permission to share in full, in part, or to refrain from sharing as they are comfortable. Remind them to "share to the center"—that is, to focus on the Christ candle at the center of the group as a reminder of God's abiding presence and sustaining help in their midst. (This also minimizes direct eye contact, making the sharing of deep feelings less difficult for the group.)

- Ask participants to take turns reading aloud their lament psalms or portions of them. Allow each person a few minutes before or after the reading to explain briefly the background of the psalm, such as what grief or loss prompted its writing.

- After each person has shared his or her lament, invite the group to pray for that person and for the petition represented in the psalm. Have participants gather around the "psalmist" and place a hand on his or her shoulder as they offer short prayers aloud. Maintain a brief silence after prayers are concluded for each person.

- To close the time of sharing laments, read the following witness to our faith:

  We believe there is no condemnation for those who are in Christ Jesus, and we know that in everything God works for good with those who love God, who are called according to God's purpose. We are sure that neither death nor life nor angels nor principalities, nor things present nor things to come nor powers nor height nor depth, nor anything else in all creation will be able to separate us from the love of God in Christ Jesus our Lord. Thanks be to God! Amen. (Adapted from Romans 8)

CLOSING (10 MINUTES)

Sing a song. Suggestions: "Jesus, Name above All Names" (TFWS) or a favorite Resurrection hymn

Read Psalm 73:21-26 slowly.

Offer a short prayer of thanks for the trust group members have placed in one another, the hope they have shown in God's faithful love, and the great gift of eternal life in Christ.

Join in this closing affirmation (leader reads the light type; group reads bold type):

Bearing it patiently,
We take up the cross;

Clinging to faith and hope,
We drink the cup of suffering;

Dropping our heavy loads,
We pick up Christ's light burden;

Savoring the joy of God,
We look fearlessly beyond death;

Knowing we are born of love,
We die trusting the Everlasting Arms.

Thanks be to God! Amen.

Say or sing a benediction.

Make an announcement. Ask each person to bring two food items to the final meeting for a closing love feast. One item should be a kind of bread that has personal symbolic meaning or a connection to fond memories. The second item will be donated to a local food pantry or ministry and may be canned or boxed.

If a second meeting is needed in order to finish sharing laments, remind the group members before they leave.

Leader's Note

Even if your group has agreed to lengthen this session or to take two weeks to share psalm laments, you will need to determine, based on the number in your group, approximately how long each person will have to share and receive prayers. Communicate this basic time frame to participants before you begin. Some psalms will be shorter than others, so actual times will vary.

Be aware that some people may be immersed in the first movement of a "petitionary psalm," the place of complaint and anger toward God. You may need to assure them that this is a natural part of the grief process and that they may experience this step several times—even for grief they thought they had already passed through. It might help to point out the psalmist's comfort in addressing God in the strongest of terms and Martha's comfort in addressing our Lord face-to-face in a rather critical manner! God can handle our anger. If participants are not yet ready to move past anger, suggest that it can help to imagine moving past it. Encourage them to look forward and to consider how they will feel when they can praise God once again. Some of the psalms are written in precisely this forward-looking mode: "Someday I will praise you." Participants can look to the faith of the psalmist or to the faith of another person who has survived great loss both for example and encouragement. Assure such persons that the group will take a faith posture on their behalf, so that what they cannot yet believe the group will believe for them.

For some members a grief may be too fresh and raw to share. They may write a psalm but be unable to speak it. Remember that sharing is always voluntary in this group. Listening to others may help such persons feel less alone. Remember too that some of us need professional help to move through certain kinds of grief, especially when the circumstances of loss are traumatic. Be alert to signs that a person may need the help of a pastoral counselor or grief therapist. Such signs include: excessive need to talk or to repeat parts of a loss story, an exaggerated sense of guilt, a high level of physical agitation or emotional volatility. Be prepared to suggest the name of a pastor or counselor who could offer a person help in moving through the grief process.

Week 9
The Gift of Restoration

PREPARATION

Prepare yourself spiritually. Read the article for Week 9, reflect on each exercise, and keep your journal. Since this will be the final meeting, pray that the group will experience a clear and satisfying sense of closure and that each participant may find meaningful ways to continue the journey in company with Christ and with one another.

Prepare materials and the room. Refer to "Weekly Needs at a Glance" to review items listed under this week's title, "The Gift of Restoration." Before the meeting, print the group response to the "Opening" prayer (Ps. 80:3) on newsprint and the "Closing" benediction on a second sheet. Select songs for the "Opening" and the love feast. If appropriate, be prepared to share any final communication with or from your partner group.

Note: Since preparation for the meeting is more complex than usual, feel free to ask group members to help you. This week you will need to arrange chairs around a large table for the love feast, which will encompass the "Deeper Explorations" time. Consider dressing the table beautifully with a cloth and perhaps fresh or dried flowers around the Christ candle. Bring several baskets or plates for the bread that will be shared and a large basket or tote bag for the donated items. Arrange in advance for donated items to be taken to a local food pantry, food bank, or other appropriate ministry (one or two group members may be glad to do this). For the "first course" of the love feast, you will need only bread in a basket or on plates. For the "second course" you will need an easily served form of fish (dried or smoked fish, canned sardines, or a cold tray of cooked shrimp with cocktail sauce). For the "third course" you will need honey and dates, grapes, or figs—common foods in Jesus' time. Have water or juice on hand to drink. You will also need a breadboard and knife, paper plates, cups, and toothpicks or utensils to suit the selected foods. Familiarize yourself with the pattern of the love feast described in the Leader's Note on page 94. Don't forget to bring your two food items.

Review the intent of this meeting: that participants recognize, as Peter did, movements of restoration in their relationship with Christ and that they have opportunity to witness to God's grace over these past nine weeks in the context of being fed at table fellowship.

OPENING (10 MINUTES)

Welcome all participants as they enter.

Set a context.

This is the final week of our journey through *The Way of Grace*. Although it is our last meeting, our faith journeys will continue all the richer for having shared this experience. Peter—the disciple who tried to follow Jesus, failed, and was restored through love—has been our traveling companion this week. Perhaps, like him, we have rediscovered in these weeks together the abundance of God's grace. This final meeting will be an opportunity to share our witness to God's grace, so we may receive strength from one another as we continue to journey forward.

Join together in worship.

- Light the candle and join in praying the "Candle Prayer," or offer words such as these: **This candle represents the light of God's love in Christ that restores us from broken promises to relationships of love and service.**

- Offer the following prayer litany, indicating to participants by gesture when it is their turn to say the refrain (posted on newsprint):

Leader: **Have mercy on me, O God,
according to your steadfast love;
according to your abundant mercy,
blot out my transgressions.**

Group: Restore us, O God;
let your face shine, that we may be saved.

Leader: **You desire truth in the inward being;
therefore teach me wisdom in my secret heart.**

Group: Restore us, O God;
let your face shine, that we may be saved.

Leader: **Create in me a clean heart, O God,**
and put a new and right spirit within me.

All: Restore us, O God;
let your face shine, that we may be saved.
(Portions of Psalms 51 and 80)

- After a few minutes of silence, invite participants to share a word or phrase that speaks to their heart without providing explanation or seeking group response.
- Sing a song. Suggestions: "Give Me a Clean Heart" (TFWS); the canon "Love, Love, Love, Love"; or "Companion Song"

SHARING INSIGHTS (45 MINUTES)

As the group members prepare to share where they have experienced God's presence this past week, remind them that this week's exercises focused on Peter's experience of grace and the theme of restoration.

1. Let participants review their notes on the article and the daily exercises for this week. Ask them to identify what spoke most deeply to them. *(5 minutes)*

2. As leader, you may wish to offer your own brief reflections first. Encourage deep and active listening. *(35 minutes)*

3. When all have shared, identify main points or common themes that have emerged, and listen for God's word to the group in these refrains. *(5 minutes)*

BREAK (10 MINUTES)

DEEPER EXPLORATIONS (50 MINUTES)

Encourage group members to witness to the grace they have received through this small-group experience, while enjoying the sustenance of food and fellowship in a love feast.

Introduce the love feast. (5 minutes)
For the remainder of our meeting we will join together in an agape meal or love feast, a wonderful way to celebrate these nine weeks together! The tradition of the agape meal is an old practice modeled on Jesus' various meals with his disciples. It is not Holy Communion but a simple reminder of how often Jesus enjoyed table fellowship and how he shared and taught through simple acts of living.

In the Moravian church, the love feast became a regular part of liturgical practice. Its pattern called for prayer and scripture reading, followed by a time of testimony in which church members witnessed to their experience of what God had done in their lives, their communities, and the world. John Wesley, among others, was moved by this pattern of worship and adopted it for use in the wider church. We will be modifying the Moravian pattern, sharing the bread we have brought and offering our witness to what God has done among us through *The Way of Grace*.

Collect the food. (5 minutes)

- Remind everyone that Jesus fed Peter before asking Peter to feed his sheep.
- Ask participants to place on the table the loaf they brought that has a symbolic significance or personal memory connection they might share later with the group. Indicate that this bread sustains all of us as we continue the journey we have shared together.
- Invite them to place the other donated food items in the basket or tote bag you brought. Explain that just as Jesus asked Peter to "feed my lambs," these gifts will feed others. Indicate the local ministry that will receive this food. Thank group members for their willingness to participate in feeding God's hungry children.

Celebrate the love feast. (40 minutes)

- Explain that the love feast celebration will have three courses of bread and other simple foods. During each course, participants will have a chance to witness to God's grace in their lives by responding to a particular question.
- Sing one or two appropriate hymns. Suggestions: "Let Us Break Bread Together," "Now Thank We All Our God," or "For the Beauty of the Earth"

Partake of the first course.

- Read Matthew 14:19-21.
- Tell the group you will offer a traditional Jewish table grace: **"Blessed are you, Lord our God, / Creator of the universe! Through your work, all things were made, / and by your goodness, we have this food to share. / Blessed be God forever."**[1] Amen.
- Distribute the first course of bread.

- Invite testimonies: **Why did you select the particular loaf you brought to this meal? How does this bread remind you of a way you have been fed—by family, by church, or by another loving presence in your life?**
- Allow time for the sharing of responses.

Partake of the second course.

- Read John 21:4-14.
- Tell the group that you will offer a prayer based on part of the early Christian teaching manual called the *Didache* (pronounced Did´-a-kay):

    We give you thanks, O God our Creator, for the path of life you have made known to us through Jesus and those who have followed in his way;
    As the grain scattered on good soil was gathered together into one loaf, so may all who continue on the way be gathered together from the ends of the earth to feast with you.[2]

- Distribute a second portion of bread along with the fish.
- Invite testimonies: **How have you experienced being fed by Christ in and through this small-group experience?**
- Allow time for the sharing of responses.
- Sing a song. Suggestions: "Sweet, Sweet Spirit" or "Amazing Grace"

Partake of the third course.

- Read John 21:15-17.
- Indicate that you will pray a traditional Moravian love feast prayer:
    Come, Lord Jesus, our Guest to be,
    And bless these gifts, bestowed by Thee.
    Bless our dear ones everywhere,
    Keep them in Thy loving care. Amen.[3]
- Distribute the final portion of bread along with fruit and honey.
- Invite testimonies: **How do you feel called to feed and serve others as an expression of your love for Jesus?**
- Allow time for the sharing of responses.

- Sing a song of commitment. Suggestions: "Jesu, Jesu" or "Take My Life and Let It Be"

CLOSING (5 MINUTES)

- Offer thanks: Invite participants to express in a sentence or two what they are most grateful to God and to one another for.
- Join in the following benediction (posted on newsprint):

Leader: **Godspeed to you and your companions as you continue this journey.**

Group: In company with one another,
and in company with God revealed to us in Jesus Christ,
we do not travel alone.

All: **We travel the way of grace.**
Let us go on!

Leader's Note

INSTRUCTIONS FOR THE LOVE FEAST

The love feast will include three courses of food. As people place their loaves on the table, divide them into three clusters, one for each course, so that by meal's end at least some of each loaf has been served. For the first course offer bread only. In the second course, serve more bread along with the fish. (Including fish in the feast is largely symbolic, so there is no need for concern if some choose not to eat it.) The third course should be the final portion of bread served with the fruit and honey. If any of the breads are sweet, serve them with this course.

Notes

Preparatory Meeting

1. Eugene H. Peterson, *Working the Angles: The Shape of Pastoral Integrity* (Grand Rapids, Mich.: William B Eerdmans, 1987), 103–104.

Week 2

1. Lines from "The Mother of Learning," in Michael E. Moynahan, *Orphaned Wisdom: Meditations for Lent* (New York: Paulist Press, 1990), 56–57.

Week 5

1. From the "Prayer for the Laying On of Hands," *The Iona Community Worship Book*, rev. ed. (Glasgow, Scotland: Wild Goose Publications, 1991), 39.

Week 6

1. Adapted from *Desert Wisdom: Sayings from the Desert Fathers* by Yushi Nomura (Garden City, New York: Doubleday & Co., 1982), 7. The word translated "self-criticism" in the book has been changed to "self-examination." Self-criticism now carries negative psychological connotations, whereas its earlier meaning was closer to honest self-examination and confession.

2. From Ann Weems, *Reaching for Rainbows: Resources for Creative Worship* (Philadelphia, Pa.: The Westminster Press, 1980), 33.

Week 9

1. From *Celebrate God's Presence: A Book of Services for The United Church of Canada* (Ontario, Canada: United Church Publishing House, 2000), 552.

2. This prayer, based loosely on a portion of the *Didache* concerning eucharistic thanks, was written by Melissa Tidwell, Editor of *Alive Now* magazine, Upper Room Ministries.

3. Moravian table grace cited on *UUCF Home Page*, clipped from "A Short Introduction to the History, Customs and Practices of the Moravian Church" by Herbert Spaugh.

Evaluation

When your group has completed *The Way of Grace* resource, please share your insights and experiences in relation to the questions below. Copy this page if you prefer not to tear it out. Use additional paper if needed.

1. Describe your group's experience with *Companions in Christ: The Way of Grace.*

2. Did the resource lead your participants to a fuller understanding and experience of God's grace in any new or concrete ways? If so, please share your perceptions with us in this evaluation or through the discussion room at www.companionsinchrist.org.

3. How could *Companions in Christ: The Way of Grace* be improved?

4. Do you have follow-up plans for your group? What resource do you plan to use, or what kinds of resources are you looking for? What other topics would you like to see in the Companions in Christ series?

Mail to: *Companions in Christ*
           Upper Room Ministries
           P. O. Box 340012
           Nashville, TN 37203-0012   or fax: 615-340-7178